Leaving my Life

A story of survival and reunion

Rut Wermuth Burak

ELSP

Published in 2010 by
ELSP
16A New St John's Road
St Helier
Jersey   JE2 3LD

Origination by Seaflower Books
Jersey

Printed by CPOD
Trowbridge, Wiltshire

ISBN 978-1-906641-19-1

© 2010 Rut Wermuth Burak

CONTENTS

	Acknowledgements	5
	Prologue	7
1	Ghetto and Death train	9
2	Return to Kolomyja	18
3	Last Goodbye	34
4	Away to Germany !	42
5	The Shoe Factory	49
6	The Maidservant Katrin	58
7	German Disasters	68
8	Arms Factory	77
9	Witek. Dilemmas of Survival	81
10	Return to a Nation Betrayed	94
11	Kolomyja– A Dream Fulfilled	100
12	Rychwald: A Search Begins	105
13	"This Man Zorza......"	112
14	Phone Calls	116
15	To London and a Brother	121
16	My Brother's Story	127
17	Memories	145
18	Bezio, Jula, Frania, and the Righteous Gentiles	154
	Epilogue	163

Hard at work with my nephew Richard

Acknowledgements

I am deeply grateful for the help and support I have received from my rediscovered family who have worked so hard, and with so much love, to help create this version of a book which I wrote originally in my native Polish.

First of all I want to thank my nephew Richard Zorza who suggested the idea of making my biography available in English and offered to work alongside me in translating it. And also my late brother's partner, Eileen Lerche-Thomsen, who has become my dear friend, who has spent many hours polishing the text that Richard and I created, and who was so determined to get it published.

Many episodes in my biography may seem difficult to believe, but so too is the story of how this version could come into existence when the author had only rudimentary English and her collaborators had not the slightest grasp of the Polish language! The method was somewhat unorthodox. After I put together the the first rough draft in my basic English, Richard had the task of turning this into readable, grammatical prose. Finally, Eileen revised it all. Most of this was done by email and during occasional visits from them to Poland or from me to USA, the UK and Jersey.

The emails flitted back and forth overseas many times, checking and re-checking to make as sure as possible that every word of the original had been properly understood and that the final draft accurately re-created the story I had to tell. It took a long time to develop the version we deliver now to the English speaking peoples of our world. I hope that this unusual, but true and moving story will catch your interest as it has done already in the Polish and German language editions.

With many thanks
Rut Wermuth Burak
Poland-Jersey-Washington
Spring 2010

"We, the Polish Jews"

"… We are not here to cry, but to light the flame undying, not of memory alone but of the continuing struggle for the victory of man over beast. For the victory of pity over cruelty, of conscience over the dark abyss…"

Julian Tuwim
20th century Polish poet

Prologue

On June 20th, 1994, I was busying myself in my little two room apartment, getting ready to leave for a few days, when the phone rang. I picked up the receiver.

"A call from abroad" said the operator. The phones in the small town were not yet directly connected to the rest of the Polish network, let alone to the worldwide network, and so international calls still came through the operator.

By now I was not surprised to be getting an international call. Since the collapse of Communism, my world had been getting larger. I already had lots of new friends. Not only in Poland, but in other countries and even on other continents. They had passed on rumours that one of my brothers had escaped to England, but that he had since died.

I waited patiently for the promised connection to 'abroad'.

Through the static and clicking a man's voice started to come through. He spoke Polish with an accent that still spoke to my heart, the sing-song intonation of the Eastern borderlands.

"Is that Rut Burak speaking?" the voice asked.

I suddenly tensed. That voice? That accent, so similar to my own?

"Speaking, Rut Burak, born Wermuth," I answered.

To this day I cannot tell you how I knew to answer at that moment in that way. I had never before introduced myself with my old and now never-used Jewish name. I never had need or reason.

There was hesitation in the man's voice. He did not seem to know what to say next, or how to say it.

"Do you know who is calling?" the question came at last.

Of course I did not know. How could I know? But I was getting a little more excited. Recently I had been corresponding with a man who had, long ago, been a school friend of my dead brother. That man's accent could maybe sound like that.

"Is this Bezio? Dov Noy from Israel?" I asked doubtfully.

"No. I am ringing from England."

Then it hit me. Somehow I knew, before any name was said. I knew no one in England. Who else could expect me to know who he was? My heart started to pound. For the first and only time in my life my hair really did stand on end.

"SALEK...?!" I screamed at the receiver.

"Salek, dearest brother, you are alive?!"

In those few words there were so many emotions. Joy, overwhelming joy. Inexpressible joy. Love. Wonder. Sadness for what had been lost. But also still a little fear, fear that this voice, both familiar and unfamiliar at the same time, would not be able to confirm my desperate hope.

"Yes, it's me, my little sister." The man answered as his voice broke into a heart-rending sob.

The operator came on, worried. "Hello, hello, what's happened? Are you there? Are you there?"

Yes, I was here, and no, nothing much had happened.

Only that after 53 years a brother and a sister had found each other. He was convinced that she had been killed in the war, and she was sure that the same had happened to him.

No, nothing at all!

Chapter 1

Ghetto and Death Train

Until 1941, I had a happy childhood. I was born in 1928, in what was then Eastern Poland, into a Jewish family which lived in Kolomyja, a small town of about 45,000 people, roughly equally divided between Jews, Poles and Ukrainians. I had a sheltered home, two older brothers, many cousins, aunts, uncles, and schoolmates. As the youngest child and the only daughter, I was pampered and loved. My two brothers Pawel and Salek spoiled and protected me. My parents owned the delicatessen, located in the main town square.

Everything changed overnight when, in September 1939, the Soviets occupied eastern Poland. Then, two years later in July 1941 came the German-Soviet war and the German invaders quickly replaced the Russians. This was the beginning of the end for us. Hitler's Holocaust destroyed our town, our culture, and our family.

The Nazis didn't waste any time before starting to impose their 'New European Order'. As soon as they had occupied the town, they plastered its walls with big posters which foretold the worst. The heading, in large capitals, proclaimed 'Death to Jews and Bolsheviks,' and below was a long list of orders and prohibitions. The penalty for failing to obey any one of them was immediate death.

All Jews were to wear the star (in our part of the county a blue star on white background), on penalty of death.

No Jews were to go to school.

Public buildings and parks were closed to Jews.

All Jews were forbidden to walk on pavements. We were required to walk in the gutter.

Day after day it got worse. Jewish businesses were closed, Jewish property was seized. Jews were forbidden to employ Gentiles. Jews were to report for forced labour.

Then the ghetto was decreed. On pain of death all Jews were to move into a small, already overcrowded, fenced in area. We were each allowed to bring only as much as we were able to carry in our two hands or in a kind of rucksack on our backs. Any Jew found outside the walls of the ghetto could be shot.

Leap for Life

Food and water were in desperately short supply. Hundreds died. But that gave us no extra space. The Germans marched Jews from the outlying villages into the ghetto, and the deaths continued.

* * *

Finally, in the early autumn of 1942, we were all ordered to the central point of the Kolomyja ghetto to be registered. We were scared, but knew no alternative. There was no registration, rather a 'selection.' There were about five thousand of us. In the middle of the square stood *"Herr"* Leideritz, the Gestapo chief of Kolomyja, with his thugs. He would point with his switch who would go to the right or the left. At the end of the process there were about three hundred people on the right, and everyone else on the left. The right meant life. My mother, my father, and I were all sent to the left.

Then they started marching us down the road.

The huge silent column, surrounded by the Ukrainian militia and a few Gestapo with German shepherd dogs, headed slowly in the direction of the railway station. It was eerily quiet. All that could be heard was the scraping of thousands of feet along the road. Occasionally you would hear the wail of a child, quickly silenced by the mother comforting it in her arms. But there were not many children or old people in the crowd. The weaker had already been killed by the terror, by the hunger, and by the diseases which had ravaged the ghetto since it had been sealed in the spring.

The streets of the town were completely deserted. But behind the tightly closed curtains you could sense the presence of happier and more privileged inhabitants, people who, unlike those now herded along in the middle of the roadway, at least thus far were being allowed to remain human beings.

Somewhere right in the middle of the crowd were the three of us holding tight to each other's hands. Mother, father and their thirteen year old daughter. We were not talking. Nobody in the crowd was talking. Yet mother, father and daughter felt each other's warmth and strength through their joined hands. We were still together – so far. It was a long way to the railway station. Perhaps a miracle would happen. Perhaps the Almighty, whom we had worshipped so often, would finally show his presence.

Although the terror had been getting worse and worse for months now, I did not fully realise what was really happening until the very end. My parents had tried all the time to keep a protective wall around me and to a certain extent they had succeeded. Our family, once five people, had now shrunk to three. I still did not know the full truth about what had happened to my brothers. I had been told that they were away,

Ghetto and Death Train

that they would soon be back, in that magical phrase "after the war." After the war all our problems would be solved. In such a time a child grows up more quickly. I had kept my eyes open and saw all too much of what was going on around me. But it was so comfortable to pretend. So easy to hide under my parents' wings and to depend on their foresight and wisdom. It had worked until now, why should it not keep working?

But there was no miracle. We came in sight of the station, but were driven further, to the loading dock. On the tracks stood a long train of cattle trucks. Their doors were wide open for loading and there was an overpowering smell from the chlorine with which the trucks had been soaked. The crowd wavered. The column which thus far had been orderly broke up and became chaotic. The area was filled with screaming, the scream of despair from five thousand throats. Did I scream too? If so, I screamed instinctively, without consciousness of what I was doing, just like everyone else there.

It seemed as if nothing could control this chaos. But suddenly there were shots and a unit of Ukrainian Militia came running up. The Militia and the Gestapo were carrying long whips with which they attacked the fear-crazed crowd. Soon they had succeeded in breaking the dense mass into individual groups next to each wagon door and the loading started.

Now hell was unleashed. The dogs barked. The whips cracked. Over the omnipresent shrieking thundered the shouted commands of the Germans and the vicious urgings of the Ukrainians: *Vorwarts, Loss, Loss, Schnell*, and *Ihr Verfluchte Judiche Schweinenhunde*. All the screaming merged into one overwhelming horror. People, trying to avoid being whipped, were climbing quickly into the wagons and helping each other, seeking the safety of the wagons – or so they thought. In wave after wave they filled the cattle trucks.

And when a truck was so full that you could not imagine another person squeezing in, a drunken Ukrainian militiaman would appear, cracking his whip to left and right and shooting his pistol. The nearest people would start climbing on top of each other to avoid being shot or whipped and suddenly a gap would appear and they would force more people into the space. They did this again and again, crowding in more and more people. How long did this last? A few hours? An eternity? Finally they managed to finish loading the wagons.

The heavy doors closed with a groan, and the sound of the doors being nailed shut confirmed the fate of the people inside. But the screaming continued from this particular 'freight shipment' and could be heard until the evening when, at last, the heavily loaded train moved off. We knew exactly where we were going.

In one of the trucks, I was with my parents. We were still together. I huddled in terror between them. In the cattle truck that could perhaps with difficulty have held fifty, perhaps eighty people, at least two hundred had been crammed. All of us, orthodox Jews with our inhibitions and prohibitions, stripped of our clothes trying to avoid the death from heat stroke that many were suffering.

My parents must have thanked God that their daughter had lost consciousness because what was going on inside those cattle cars was beyond anyone's worst imaginings of the Day of the Last Judgment. The screaming, the stench, the chlorine stinging nose and lungs. I was suffocating, falling into unconsciousness, then waking again to the screams, the banging of the wheels and the sudden shots. How long had it been going on? I did not know. I had blacked out.

Somehow, when I regained consciousness, I became aware that my parents were still near me, that with their strongly intertwined arms they had made with their bodies a tent protecting me from the crush. It was only thanks to them that I was still alive. We were standing naked, pressed against each other and against the wooden side of the cattle truck, which was the only reason that we still had some air to breathe. Those in the middle were no longer alive, but their bodies were still upright. It was impossible for them to fall or even slide to the floor.

When I next came round, I felt a breath of air. There seemed to be a little space around us. I heard Mama whispering in my ear.

"Listen carefully to what I have to say. Some of the young people have managed to tear out a plank from the side of the wagon and now they are jumping out. We have decided to do the same. We may die this way, but if we stay we know we will die. Dad will go first, then you, and last me. We are going through a forest now. It is night. When you land, run to the forest and hide there. Don't worry, we will find you later."

Before I had a chance to realise what was going on, strong hands grasped me under my arms, lifted me up, and pushed me through the gap in the side of the truck. I hung there, still supported by the unknown hands under my arms. I felt the air rushing

Ghetto and Death Train

past. At last I could breathe. I came properly to my senses. Suddenly the hands which had been holding me let me go. I was flying into the bottomless dark.

Bitter cold forced me back into consciousness. I could see that the sky was growing light. But for a long time I could not recollect where I was, or what was happening to me. At last, slowly, very slowly, the terrible reality surfaced in my memory. I moved my limbs, confirming that my arms and legs were intact, but I had a terrible headache and could see through only one eye. When I lifted my hand to my head I felt something warm and sticky. From an injury a slow stream of blood trickled, covering my eyes. This was why I could not see.

It was nearly dawn. I began to notice the rustle of the trees and the birds, singing out their frenzied joy at the awakening new day. To those winged creatures the only important thing was that sunrise was coming again, and as with every dawn, their little throats were full of song to celebrate the everyday miracle of nature. They did not care about the war of these petty humans who could not fly. They did not care about those killed, not by the laws of nature, but out of wanton enjoyment of killing.

I realised with surprise that I was in the middle of the forest and that the railway tracks were nowhere to be seen. I had no memory of how I had got there. Maybe one of the others who escaped had noticed that I was unconscious and had dragged me away from the most dangerous area. Suddenly my heart beat more strongly. Perhaps it was my parents who had saved me. Perhaps they would soon appear from behind a tree and take everything into their good, strong hands and everything would be as before. But those were just wild hopes. From now, nothing would ever be the same. I was in this forest alone, and thrown only on my own resources.

I did not move from that spot for a long time. The birds grew silent, offering only occasionally a single late trill. I tore up some grass and used it to rub off the coagulating blood, which still dripped slowly, and got to my feet. I knew I could not go on standing there for ever. I had to make a decision. But what could I do? I was naked, bruised all over and bleeding. Many a time as a child I had had a terrible dream, that I alone was naked among other people properly dressed, that I was trying to run to escape, but that I was paralysed and could not move. Then I would wake and feel the huge relief that this was only a dream. Now, from this, there was no awakening. If people saw me, they would guess on the spot who I was, and where I had come from. Wouldn't they betray me to the Germans?

At last I moved. I slipped from tree to tree, crouching under bushes. I do not know how far I went. Finally I reached the edge of the forest. Beyond there was a narrow path at the end of which stood a small cottage with a straw roof. Smoke was rising from the chimney. There must be someone at home. I held back in the cover

Leap for Life

of the forest, and watched the hut, hesitating for ages and wondering if I dared knock on the door. I really had no choice, and plucking up all my courage I forced myself to run into the open towards the hut. I was nearly there when suddenly the door opened and a woman appeared, carrying buckets. She dropped them with a clatter and a loud scream, making the sign of the cross over her breast. Maybe she thought she had seen a ghost. She would not have been far wrong.

Hearing the scream, a man rushed out from the doorway. They were both somewhat elderly. I tried to talk, wanting to explain to them as quickly as possible where I had appeared from. But my voice would not come out of my constricted throat. My words were low and trembling. They looked at me in disbelief. At last they started to understand. They pulled me indoors and into a dark passageway, fastening the door from the inside with a bar.

"Just give me something to wear, perhaps only an old shirt, and I will go away from here," I was pleading.

"Oh, my poor *detyno!*" (Ukrainian for child) The woman suddenly gave way to tears.

"Bring some milk," she ordered her husband. He disappeared into what must have been the kitchen, coming back with an earthenware cup full of hot milk. I took it in my trembling hands and drank greedily, burning my lips. I felt the healing warmth spreading through my veins.

Then the woman disappeared. She came back with a long, somewhat worn linen shift. I slipped it on, as happy as if she had given me the richest gown in whole world, as indeed it was. It was a gift from the heart. That these two poor people should decide to give a child something that must have been very valuable to them in the difficulties of wartime was a sign that human kindness had not yet completely disappeared from the world. But it was not until much later that I was to think in this way. The woman said:

"You can't stay here long. Our sons will be back soon. I'm not sure that they would be pleased to find you here. Go to the town. There are still Jews there. They will help you."

She came with me to the road.

"This will take you to the railway line. Follow it and you will come to the town. *Z Bohom, detyno* (God be with you, child)."

I wanted to hug her, but I did not dare. I stuttered some thanks and moved off quickly in the direction she was pointing.

From the peasants' hut, I followed the path through the field, holding up the shift that was too big for me. I reached the tracks. There were people walking backwards and forwards along them, as if searching for something. When I got closer I could see

Ghetto and Death Train

that they were wearing armbands with the star of David. One of them noticed me. He gazed at my shift, at my injured head. He knew immediately.

"You escaped from the night train, didn't you?" He was confirming rather than asking.

"We are looking for people like you. Do you know of any others?"

"I know that several people jumped from our truck. My mother and father too. But I haven't met anybody. I don't know what has happened to them."

They had brought a bundle of clothes with them. They knew what condition the escapees were in. They wrapped some clothes about me. One of them took me by the hand and led me to the town. It was not far away.

He went into one of the cottages. We went through a dark area towards a bright room. There were a few beds and along the wall there were rows of straw-filled mattresses. Moaning, injured people were lying on them.

I was standing and looking around when suddenly, from one of the straw mattresses, I heard a low voice, muffled by a bandage.

"Rutka!?"

I turned as if struck by a thunderbolt. It was Mama's voice. I could hardly recognize her. She had grown older and grey in one night.

We collapsed weeping into each others arms. We could not utter even one word.. I embraced her carefully so as not to hurt her. She was in much worse condition than me. One question, just one question, kept hammering in my mind. For a long time I could not bring myself to ask it. But Mama knew what I was thinking and answered my unspoken question. She realised that she could no longer hide the truth, the way she and my father had done when my brothers had vanished. Now things had gone too far. Our future was totally unknown. In spite my young age, I was now grown up, and I had to know.

"Dad is dead. They shot him when he jumped. I saw it with my own eyes."

We did not cry. There is a limit to people's endurance. We were close to it, we had run out of tears.

The Jewish community of the small town tried to help us as much as they could. They found us the clothes we needed. The most badly injured got medical care and the rest of us were placed with the better off families, although by now almost all of them were poor too. In this town there was not yet a separate ghetto. Mama and I stayed with one of the families who offered their help. Here in the *shtetl* (Yiddish for a small town) the family accepted us under their roof and shared with us what they had, although they themselves had very little. They were in fear, as we all were.

Then a rumour began to circulate that the *shtetl* would soon be made *Judenrein*

Leap for Life

– free of Jews. Everyone knew exactly what that would mean. It became clear to us that we could no longer stay with this family.

Then one day Mama came in very excited. She had found out that in a nearby estate the *Treuhander* (the German estate administrator) was looking for a maid. "I want to try to get this job," she declared. She needed to look the part and set about it energetically. Our hosts were very helpful in putting together an outfit of peasant's clothes, a white gathered skirt, a hand embroidered linen shift, a bright headscarf and a ribbon around her neck with a Madonna pendant hanging from it. I waited with a little hope and great anxiety to see how this disguise would fare.

Mama went off to the *Treuhander*. She was one of several applicants. In broken Polish and Ukrainian, which provided good camouflage for her slight Yiddish accent, she started to list her virtues, how modest she was, how honest she was, how clean she was, and what a good cook she was.

"Before the war, I served a wealthy Jewish family in Lwow. The husband was a well known doctor. They did a lot of entertaining. My mother gave me to them when I was a young girl and I learned everything there. I can cook and bake and I know how to keep an upper class home."

This tipped the balance. The *Treuhander* needed someone like that. They took her on even though she had no identity papers, agreeing that she could bring them later. Mama would have a corner of the kitchen to sleep in, and her board. As for salary, they would discuss it after they had seen what she could do. She was to start early in the morning the next day.

It had worked! Very pleased with herself, she came back shortly before curfew. Yes, but what about me? What would happen next? What about the papers that she just did not have? All that night we sat in our corner on the straw pallet, which was brought out only at bedtime, and talked feverishly about what to do next. Shortly before morning, we had settled everything.

"You go back to our old house and to Frania, back to Kolomyja and our maid. I left a little money with her and some jewellery. Maybe we can use this to get some papers for me. Maybe we can find shelter for you. Maybe you can manage to get there and back safely." Since Frania was not Jewish, when we were forced into the ghetto she had taken over the share of our apartment that the Russians had left us.

Maybe, maybe! Behind every 'maybe' there were hidden deadly fears. We knew that the route was full of possible ambushes. We knew that death could be lying in wait every minute and at every corner. But did we have any other choice? We simply had to try. If we just kept passively waiting it would only end in death. And this way there was at least some chance of survival. So we had to take it, and we did.

It was still dark when Mama began to get ready. She got together her few possessions and tied them into a bundle using a scarf. She had said goodbye to our kind hosts the day before when they had insisted she accept a little money. Most of these coins she knotted into a handkerchief. They were for my train ticket. We stood embracing without words for a long time. Then she left, quietly closing the door after her. I watched through a chink in the curtains as she vanished around the next corner. Would I ever see her again?

I had to go too. I put on the only dress I had. It had vertical stripes and reached below the knee. I plaited my hair, which had grown longer in the meantime, into two stiff braids. On my feet I had old, ill-fitting shoes. Our hosts examined me carefully. "You look the perfect *shicksa*. We are sure you will carry it off. Here is a piece of bread and some small change for your trip. Take it. Take it! We know that Mama could not give you much and you don't know what may happen on the way. And when you get back, come and see us."

I went. The pale autumn sun was already over the horizon. From all the chimneys came wisps of smoke. Breakfast was on the stove. The *shtetl* lay quiet and remote. It was as peaceful as if there were no war or insanity in the world.

Chapter 2

Return to Kolomyja

I had to walk a few miles to Bukaczowce where I would catch a train. Today there was to be a market in the town. As I walked along at the side of the road, horse-drawn carts passed me, driven by peasants, some accompanied by their wives wrapped up tightly in shawls against the cold. They were bringing their own produce to sell at the market. Suddenly one of the carts slowed down and a gruff voice called out in Ukrainian, "Where are you going? To the market? Come on up and I will drive you."

I was not at all happy about the idea. I was afraid of having any contact with people. But what could I do? To reject such an offer could be suspicious too. So I jumped into the cart with words of thanks. *"Wio Maluskie!"* "Gee up!" My benefactor flicked the whip. Only three quarters of an hour later I was in the town.

I wandered around and then made for the railway station. I queued up at the window and was soon the proud owner of a ticket to Kolomyja. "You see how simple it is." I said to myself, trying to build up the courage I needed so badly. "Now both Mama's fate and mine depend on my decisions and how I put them into action. I must not be afraid."

The station clock showed 11 am. The train to Stanislawow, where I had to change, was not due to leave until 2 pm. I was afraid to stay at the station, where there were a lot of dubious looking characters. So I went back to the market, which was noisy and crowded, and where I thought I would be safer. I was wandering back and forth, pretending to be looking for something to buy, when suddenly I heard an uproar. "Run! Germans!!" Like everyone else, I started to run. But it was too late. A military column surrounded the square and with German efficiency searched through all the carts and baskets. Fortunately, this time they were more interested in merchandise than in people. The square was filled with the lamentations of women whose butter, cheese and eggs had been taken. Suddenly the Germans left as quickly as they had come. They left a scene of devastation, with all the food they had not wanted stamped into the mud, all done just for the pleasure of it.

I breathed a sigh of relief and ran quickly to the station because it was almost time for the train. Soon I was standing in the very crowded corridor of the train which set off for the town of Stanislawow. If I was lucky, I would be 'home' in Kolomyja before curfew.

At this time, trains were not very punctual and every journey was an unknown adventure. Our train stopped somewhere along the track without any obvious reason. Anxious not to miss my connection to Kolomyja, I leant out of the window and noticed some movement near the engine. Sacks were being thrown out. Suddenly we were off again at full speed, but not before I had caught a glimpse of figures wearing caps and long boots emerging from the forest. It was easy enough to guess that the engine driver was in league with the resistance fighters. For me this incident had one serious consequence - I missed my connection. The next train to Kolomyja would not leave until the following morning.

I was in a dilemma again. What should I do? I already knew that to stay at the station would be very dangerous because the Ukrainians and Germans often conducted roundups in such public places. And operating on the edges of the roundups there were always the *szmalcownicy*, blackmailers, who would threaten to expose Jews and who hunted for people like me. The waiting room was full of people sleeping on the floor. Suddenly I heard whispering. "Who would like to stay overnight? Who?" A young man in a railway uniform was going from group to group asking this question. I tugged at his sleeve. "How much to stay for the night?" He mentioned a price. In my mind I counted my meagre resources. "OK" I quickly decided.

It was already dark. He led me through narrow streets and courtyards which only he knew. At last he opened a door and we went into a dark stairwell. It smelt of sauerkraut. The smell released my hunger, which had been suppressed all day by my fear. One floor up he unlocked a door. A young woman, obviously his wife, looked at me dubiously. Who had he brought this time, her eyes seemed to ask?

"Do you have money for the overnight stay?" she asked. I quickly pulled out my coins, making sure to give a little more than they had asked.

"Do you travel without luggage?"

"Yes"

"All right." she waved with her hand, carefully counting the coins.

"You can lie down there," pointing to a pallet on the floor.

Suddenly, in the other corner of the room, something whimpered. The woman went over to the baby's cot, and, murmuring calmly and caressingly, took out her full white breast to quiet the baby. I squatted down on my pallet and took out a crust of bread.

"Wait, I will make you some tea," she said.

Leap for Life

She put the baby back in his cot and went to the kitchen stove. She made me a cup of hot linden tea. I felt somewhat better. The waves of warmth went through my body and my fear seemed slowly to melt away. I slept.

Suddenly in the middle of the night I was woken by a squeak of the bed. I lifted my head to look. They were lying together. The railwayman and his young wife. I had never before seen a grown man and woman sleeping together in the same bed. At first I did not understand what was going on, but slowly I worked it out.

This was how I learned about sex. I put together into a logical whole what I had heard whispered in school corners. I recalled the grins of the older girls when they had spoken about 'it'. At home we never spoke about 'it' To talk to the children about 'such things' was not the way things were done in a good middle class family. But I already knew that it was not the stork who brought children. During the period of Russian occupation one of the teachers at our school had been pregnant. Before the occupation she would never have been allowed to continue teaching. But this was one of the changes, together with co-educational schools, that the Soviets introduced. Her prominent belly was a perpetual source of giggles and fluster from us girls. "So they did 'it' this way, yes, that is repulsive," was all I could think before I went back to sleep.

In the morning I was woken by loud whispering.

"You know, I do not like that girl. She is travelling all on her own without any luggage. Perhaps she is Jewish?"

"Shhh! She'll hear you! No, I don't think she is. I looked her over carefully. After all, she paid you, didn't she? Anyway, she'll be going soon," I heard her husband reassure her.

I was rigid with fear. For a long time I pretended to be deeply asleep. When at last I opened my eyes, the woman was busy near the kitchen stove preparing breakfast for her husband who seemed ready to go to his shift. I got up quickly and got dressed.

"Let's go," he said.

He led me back to the railway station and put me on the direct train to Kolomyja. I had been lucky again. It appeared there had been another roundup during the night. Just two hours later the train was pulling into the station back in my home town of Kolomyja.

As I got out I quickly pulled my scarf tighter over my head, realising that here someone was much more likely to recognise me. Then I started marching homewards, towards what was no longer my home. It was a long way from the station, and as I got closer I started to walk more and more slowly, for I did not know what was awaiting me, and how Frania would greet me. Would she let me down? So many others, who

Return to Kolomyja

had seemed honest and trustworthy had already done so. And what would I do if she would not help? I had no money, no other place to stay, and there was no way I could buy a ticket back. Frania was my only hope.

Now every step I took reminded me of the past. The post office on the left, and next to it the old pre-war government office, near the Mars Cinema. And soon I saw that familiar balcony from which I had so often watched the busy street life below. My eyes filled with tears. But no. I could not allow myself to cry. I had to be strong. Mama was still alive and now on her own. She was waiting for me. I could not disappoint her.

In the town square opposite our house whirled a colourful crowd. At market stalls, heart-shaped ginger cakes and strings of onions and garlic were on sale. There were also piles of mushrooms, vegetables and fruit. There was loud haggling because, despite the apparent abundance, black market prices were high and few of the customers could afford to buy much. In the shops there was nothing and the ration cards did not provide enough to survive.

I watched, surprised at the ordinary everyday bustle. So people could still live like this. I had already forgotten what it was like. It seemed to me that I was on a strange planet. Just one month ago you could have seen the walls which enclosed the ghetto from this market place, the walls which so completely and efficiently had divided not only physical space but also acted as the frontier between two different worlds. Between life and annihilation. And I had been living behind those walls. Now the ghetto did not exist any more. A part of it was set on fire, the walls were pulled down and the houses, almost warm from their poor prior occupants, were settled by new people, by people who enjoyed the right to go on living.

I walked up and down in the town square for a long time, unable to bring myself to go to our old house. What if someone recognised me? What if Frania did not live there any more? I was only just beginning to realise how dangerous the whole scheme was.

Suddenly someone grabbed my shoulder.

Without thinking I lifted my head and the headscarf slid down from my hair. A tall, strong-boned woman looked intently at me.

"Rutka?"

"Paulina?"

We cried out almost in unison. The woman quickly slid the scarf back into place, pulling it well forward to hide my face, and drew me aside.

"Lets go. This is no place for you!"

"But I'm going to Frania," I insisted.

Leap for Life

"Not now. Now you shouldn't. It's full daylight and there are lots of people around. I'll take you to the Targowica, and then we'll contact Frania."

For me, this was a real piece of luck. Targowica, on the outskirts of Kolomyja, consisted of very poor homes which had straw roofs and often only hard earth floors. It was a long way from the centre of the town, close to the banks of the river Prut. It took its name from the wide open area in which was held a market every week selling horses and other domestic animals. It was almost like a separate village. Only the poorest of the poor lived there, Ukrainians, often three generations living together in one room and the families had many, many children. Ducks and geese wandered in the muddy courtyards with the cock lording it over his harem of hens. In the ramshackle pigsties, put together with odds and ends, piglets squealed, and from huts with hearts carved into the woodwork wafted the smell of clover.

Against this background, Paulina's cottage stood out proudly. It was whitewashed and in the windows were brilliant flame-red geraniums. In the hallway stood two barrels, one filled with water and the other with sauerkraut. From one side of the hallway, you entered the kitchen. The kitchen had a big oven in which you could cook a meal and bake bread, and on which you could even sleep. Such stoves were characteristic of Carpathian villages.

On the other side of the hall was the living room with a well-swept earth floor. This had to be coated each week with a special yellow clay to keep it clean. Holy pictures of Mary, and of Jesus, with a fiery heart surrounded with a crown of thorns, hung on the whitewashed walls.

Below them was a broad bench covered by a wonderfully coloured *Hucul*[1] rug, known as a *kilim*, and piled on it, in order of size with the smallest on top, about half a dozen cushions. A very deep cupboard, a chest, a scrubbed-white wooden table and four sturdy wooden chairs completed the furniture. Along the walls were shelves with coloured pottery bowls and cups painted in the *Hucul* pattern. White embroidered curtains hung at the small square windows and the sills were covered with flower-filled pots.

How well I remembered this room from the time before the war. I loved it. Just for a moment I forgot what I had become, forgot that now all this pride, tidiness and neatness was no longer for me. Not for me the white curtains and the red geraniums. And indeed Paulina pointed me into the darkest corner of the hallway, a kind of a pantry behind a curtain.

---

[1] The Hucul are a highland tribe who live in the Carpathian Mountains (now on the Ukraine-Romania border). They have a rich and varied culture, especially known for their colourful folk costume, handmade cross-stitch embroidery, rugs, pottery and woodwork."

"Sit in there and don't show yourself or make a sound, whatever happens. Nobody must guess that you are there. In the meantime I will get in touch with Frania and together we will consider what to do next."

She brought me a cup of hot milk and a thick chunk of home-made bread, and a blanket with which I made myself a cosy nest. She locked the door to the house from the outside with a padlock and left me.

The meal tasted heavenly. To make it last, I chewed every mouthful and sipped the milk slowly. Then I lay down. It was a long time since I had felt so comfortable and relaxed. I wasn't so desperately lonely any more. Here was someone else to help me act and make decisions. I fell into a numb state of half sleep. Outside I could hear the noises of the yard, the cackling hens, the squeals of the piglets and dogs barking in the distance. But all this gradually faded away and behind my eyelids I began to see pictures of my lost childhood.

Who was Paulina? She spoke Polish fairly well, in addition to her native Ukrainian. She also knew some words of Yiddish. At our home, when the holidays approached and the big clean up that came with them, then it was time to go to the Targowica to get Paulina. That was always the job of my adored older brother Salek. Mama insisted that I was too small to go so far by myself, but I never wanted to miss the excitement. I loved going to fetch Paulina. At her home everything seemed so different.

Salek generally gave in to my pleas and took me with him. But I had to promise not to dawdle because he always had very important things of his own to take care of too. Salek was always in a hurry and wanted to see about his boys-only business at the same time. So he quickly told Paulina what she had to be told, agreed the terms with her, and then ran off to his Ukrainian schoolmate, whose home was in this neighbourhood. They both went to school in the local *gymnasium* (high school). The boy was talented, but he came from a very poor family and it was not easy for him to manage in such an elite school. Salek, who was already very sensitive to social problems, tried to help him. They always had various schemes going which they invariably kept secret from me, a mere little girl.

So I would spend the time at Paulina's, which made me very happy. I was treated as a special visitor, and that made me so proud. She made me sit down ceremonially on the bench below the holy pictures. From the deep chest she brought out aniseed-flavoured cakes. Then there was raspberry cordial, or tea, whatever we wanted. She sat down beside me and we had long 'adult' talks. I was deeply touched by this. At that time everyone else treated me like a child.

A few days later she would appear at our place in Pilsudski Street, and get on with the job, whatever it was, laundry or window cleaning or floor polishing. I did

Leap for Life

not realise then what hard work it was. For whatever Paulina did, she did with such grace that she made it seem easy. She seemed to treat work more as a kind of ritual celebration, than as a task to be borne.

When what we called 'the big laundry' was being done, I liked to stay in the kitchen. The familiar room, wreathed in steam, took on a completely different appearance. Laundry bubbled in a metal pan on the stove. The kitchen was dominated by a large round wash-tub supported on four stools in the centre of the room. Paulina stood at the tub in an embroidered linen shirt, with her sleeves rolled up high and with her voluminous skirt tucked up. With her strong arms plunged up to the elbows in soapy water, she skilfully rubbed the linen on the tin washboard.

I was fascinated most of all by the wringing-out. I watched carefully how completely she wrung out the water from the sheets, the bed covers and the table cloths, changing them into long white snakes. During the rinsing, she repeated this several times. At the end she had to treat the washing with starch and blue whitener. She added to the water a blue powder which 'added whiteness'. I found this illogical. I could not understand why a dark blue powder should bleach washing. At the very end, the white snakes were spread out with a loud smack, and hung up in the attic to dry. And in a few days it was time for the second stage, the ironing.

Mama was always keen to buy all the latest technical novelties. So she had bought an electric iron too, one of the very first which appeared on sale. But Paulina was completely against such gadgets.

"This is meant to be used for ironing? Never!"

So she worked in the old way, using a heavy iron loaded with glowing charcoal, until the laundry became smooth and shiny. After a few hours of ironing, Paulina got a headache from the fumes and wrapped a wet towel around her head and lay down on Frania's bed to relax.

Best of all I liked to listen to the talk when Paulina and Frania settled down for afternoon tea or coffee, followed by a snack of shortcakes. And what talk it was! There was gossip about other households and their habits. (Tactfully, in my presence, they omitted discussion of our establishment.) They talked about Christian holidays, information which was to prove so useful to me later on. They commented on the message of the Sunday sermon which was "so beautiful, my dear, that I had to cry." But most interesting of all were the tales of ghosts and miracles, which sent shivers down my spine and which "no doubt, my dear, really happened" – sometimes eyewitnesses were even quoted.

Frania subscribed to *Rycerz Niepokalanej*, a Catholic weekly for the masses, and so she seemed to me to be a very well informed person. For me, who was just starting school, and for Paulina who was almost illiterate despite speaking three languages and certainly being an intelligent woman, Frania was an authority never to be questioned or challenged.

Our Frania! She was a very important member of the family, and for us children, the first resort. Of course, our parents were there, but we felt at a greater distance from them. It was Frania to whom you ran with a scraped knee or a bruise or any other childhood disaster. She always had a solution for everything. The scraped knee she treated with iodine. The best medicine for a bruise was to hold a wide knife firmly against it. For a cut the best treatment was to cover it in the well-washed leaf of a special herb called *goby*. We firmly believed in her medicine – and it worked. It was always Frania who was waiting with a warm and tasty meal when each of us, savagely hungry, arrived back home at our various times. It was to her we told of our successes and failures. Mama was busy from dawn to dusk with the shop and did not have time for our childish problems

* * *

I don't know whether my daydream lasted for one hour, or several, but suddenly I could hear the scratch of a key at the door. Bewildered, I brought myself back to the present and got to my feet. My hearing, sensitised by fear, made everything louder. This time, fortunately, there was no need for fear. The door opened and there appeared...Frania. Forgetting Paulina's careful instructions I leapt into her broad arms, opened in a gesture of welcome.

Behind her, Paulina did not forget the warnings. She carefully closed the door, pulled the curtains tight, since outside an early autumn dusk was falling, and lit the paraffin lamp. (The benefits of civilisation had not yet reached the Targowica.) We followed her into the room where Frania examined me intently in the flickering lamplight.

"You have changed," she told me at last. "You are no longer the carefree child I knew so well. And now, sit down and tell us everything. I know only that the three of you were seen in the crowd that was driven to the railway station. It was after the roundup of the ghetto. I have heard what happened to everyone and have already mourned you."

I started to tell my tragic story. They did not interrupt me. Only the tightening grip of their hands, holding firmly to mine, and the tears running down their cheeks told how intently they were listening. The flickering of the lamp made shadows on the walls and the room filled with memories of my beloved family, Dad, Pawel, Salek – all gone. Mama! I shook myself back to reality.

"Only the two of us are left now after our escape. She is waiting for my help. I cannot fall to pieces. I have to be strong and grown up."

But could we get away with it? Would we manage to evade the pack of bloodhounds that were after us. At this very moment I was safe within the hospitable walls of this home. I could sense the sympathy of these two women, and could believe they were our friends. But were they, in fact? And to what extent could I really depend on their help in this world full of wolves? They knew, as I did, that if they agreed to help us, they would be endangering their safety, even their lives. Could we ask this of them? But was there any other way out of the trap that surrounded us? Was there any other way of cheating the precise, well tuned Nazi killing machine?

It was already very late in the evening. The first person to break the silence was Frania. She hugged me hard and kissed me. It seemed as if she had read my unexpressed thoughts and gave an immediate answer.

"I don't yet know how we'll pull it off, but you can count on my help. I can't take you with me. In your old house, on the second floor is the *Deutsche Haus,* a kind of officers club, and I work there as the caretaker. I think that for two or three days you can stay here." Now she looked intently at Paulina, who after some hesitation, at last nodded her head firmly, then went to busy herself in the kitchen.

"During that time I'll try to make money selling some of the goods which Mama left. Then we can think through what to do next. Now it's time to go to bed. Curfew has long passed. I'll sleep here tonight and in the morning we'll get started."

Meanwhile Paulina had lit the fire in the kitchen stove and warmed up a large kettle of water, which she poured into a tub.

"And now get out of your rags. I will wash them tomorrow" she said, handing me a piece of grey soap, "and scrub yourself." I plunged with delight into the hot water. How long had it been since I had last had a bath?

In the ghetto there had been no such luxury. Not only because of the cramped living situation, in which many, many people shared a room, but above all because water itself was so short. The few wells soon ran dry and at the pumps there were always huge queues. Even there the Germans often took over, scaring people away just for their own amusement. So water was rationed very harshly, and often there was none, even to drink. If we did manage to get any, we hoarded it like the great treasure which it really was to us.

While I had my bath in the kitchen, a big pot of potatoes had been gurgling on the stove. The smell of bacon fat and onion permeated the room. My goodness, what a smell! I could not stay a minute longer in the tub, although it had been very pleasant there. I jumped out and rubbed my skin clean with the rough linen towel till it glowed

Return to Kolomyja

pink. And in a moment, dressed in Paulina's much too large embroidered *soroczka* or shirt, I was sitting with the two women at the table. In front of me materialized a mountain of mashed potatoes richly dressed with fatty gravy, and next to it a cup of delicious sour milk with a thick head of yellow cream. They did not have to invite me twice to tuck into such a feast! I stuffed myself until my ears trembled, as the old Polish saying goes.

"And now to bed," Frania ordered when I finished. "Tomorrow morning early you have to hide yourself in your den again. Paulina will tidy up everything here so that there is no trace that a stranger has been here, and I will return to Pilsudski Street."

She was careful not to say "to my house." I valued the delicacy in her choice of words. The two tiny attic rooms on the third floor where she now lived, and everything inside it – were all that remained of what used to be our large flat.

In 1939 when this part of Poland was overrun by the Soviets, they considered us as 'bourgeois'. The Reds, as we called them, took the shop away from us, and the flat as well, leaving only this small top floor, where all six of us were cooped up, including Frania, of course, for she was part of the family too. She would have been free to move away and live in better circumstances, for she belonged to the 'exploited classes' but evidently she had decided not to exercise this 'privilege'. Not so Adolf, our shop assistant. He very willingly took the position of manager of our shop when the new rulers offered it to him. Our parents were very hurt. They would have preferred a stranger to take over. But he had the job for less than two years before he suffered the same repression as all other Jews when the Nazis displaced the Reds.

From that period, I remembered very clearly the evening ritual of turning our little room, which had once been the nursery, into our common sleeping room. In one corner stood a green iron bed. Since they had not allowed us to take any furniture this was one of a pair of very old ones, taken down from the loft. Mama slept here. At its foot stood a small sofa which served as a couch during the day, and at night as my bed. Dad slept on an armchair which folded out, and the boys on the table…yes, the table! The big family table was lengthened with a small children's desk, upholstered with feather cushions, and that made a bed for my brothers. Frania slept in the kitchen on the other green bed. She had the luxury of sleeping alone in the only other available space.

Despite the lack of space and the ever worsening living conditions (which you would have to call luxurious in the light of what happened when the Germans came) Salek and I liked this temporary situation. We thought of it as camping, a kind of holiday. We did not really believe that it would be much longer until everything would get back to normal. Pawel, at 18, considered himself an adult and was already

27

walking out with a girlfriend. This, in turn, for Salek and me was an inexhaustible source of fun. We teased him constantly, and he didn't like it. He took his courting very seriously and was, presumably, really in love. As far as we could tell, Frania was better informed about the affair than Mama.

I, particularly, did not realise how serious things were becoming for us. Rather, we were happy to be much closer to our parents. Our father spent most of his time sitting at home. He read a lot. I remember him browsing through a volume of Marx's *Das Kapital*. Perhaps he wanted to understand better what "those Reds" were up to.

Mama, as always, was the more active. She was forever coming and going, trying to arrange something or other. She was busy, probably making deals, because we had to have something to live on. Through our cramped flat each day passed many people, all strangers as far as I knew. Sometimes they were even Russian Red Army officers, *Komandirs*. Usually after their visits we would have to go and sleep away from home. Now I realise that they came to warn us about deportations to Siberia. This was when the word *razzia*, round-up, first appeared in our vocabulary. The Russians would arrive at night. People were given only a few minutes to pack before leaving under guard. They rounded up mainly Poles, but also some Jews. It was the NKVD who decided the criteria for deportation.

But, on the whole, life was not so bad. I think my parents had succeeded in rescuing some of our goods such as flour, sugar, canned meat and fish, particularly tinned sardines. Mama had managed to store all these items in safe places with honest people before the expropriation of our property. At least that was what she intended. How was she to know how quickly the meanings of 'honesty' and 'honour' would become devalued?

What we proudly called our 'apartment house' stood in the very centre of the town. On the ground floor there were shops, above were the formal rooms with their so-called "Venetian" windows and balconies, and the final floor was, strictly speaking, a kind of attic. There the back walls of the kitchen and the nursery were attached to a long and narrow pantry, with a mansard roof. The pantry had no windows, only a round skylight. Depending on need, it could be left open or be closed with a metal cover. The pantry was for me the goal of mysterious expeditions and investigations. I loved to explore its dark corners, to peer out through the round hole in the roof at the sky with its swimming clouds, with their constantly changing appearance, and to dream about their shapes. Most of all I liked it when one of the boys would lift me up high so I could get a view through the gap. I could see a sea of roofs and far below the statue of Pilsudski and the Town Hall. From this vantage point everything appeared somehow different and mysterious. But it happened very rarely, because it was forbidden by our parents. They were afraid for our safety.

In one corner of this pantry stood a big old-fashioned cupboard with a huge bottom drawer. I can still remember its smell of naphthalene and calamint, which seemed to protect clothes against moths. I often used it to play hide and seek. Before the war, in the summer, furs, winter clothes and other oddments were stored there. In that very cupboard, during the Russian occupation we had hidden some of our stores. Other clever hiding places had been made in the pantry. Some of the goods were still there now, and were the basis of my mother's hopes, and of my own. And this was also what was in Frania's mind when she spoke of getting money, which we needed so desperately.

I stayed four days at Paulina's place. I moved around in the main room only at night, when I was sure that nobody would drop in. During this time Frania was running all over the place selling the things Mama had stored. While the items were very much in demand at that time, it was neither easy nor safe to sell them. But at last she managed and on the third evening she came in with the harvest of yet one more deal.

"So," she began, after we had made sure that the windows were closed and covered, "I have some clothes here for you. A warm grey and white checkered woollen wrap and a set of plain linen underwear. I found a pair of your ski boots in the cupboard. I hope you have not grown out of them. They are strong and good quality, so you should be able to wear them for a long time to come. And look, here under the inner sole I have put in three little pictures from your childhood, wrapped into a parchment paper. I have thought hard about whether you should take them, because they might put you in danger. But I think you should have them, and your mama should decide if you should keep them with you. Your dark blue school overcoat is still there, but you couldn't get away with wearing clothes like that now. You've got to look like a peasant girl. So instead we'll keep you in the wrap, and in the clothes that you arrived in. The striped dress is not so

One of the hidden photos taken when I was about three

Leap for Life

bad, and Paulina is washing it and getting it ready."

"But, the most important thing of all is this," she said, passing me a small prayer book, a rosary in a little tin box, and a metal cross to go round my neck. "You have to learn the prayers so well that you can reel them off by heart, even in the middle of the night, when you awaken from a deep sleep. And forget your name. From now on you are Katarzyna Raduga, born in Tarnopol, the daughter of Franciska Raduga and an unknown father."

I knew the story of Kasia very well, although I had never met her myself. When Frania was still a very young girl, she had been taken advantage of and then abandoned by a man whose name she had never ever mentioned. At that time to be an unmarried woman with a child was a cause for great shame. It would be hard to describe what awful things she experienced before eventually deciding to leave her daughter, then six years old, with her relatives in Tarnopol to go to look for work in another town. That was how she had ended up in Kolomyja. The world had not been kind to her. She had wandered a long way before finding shelter with us. I was five years old when she came.

To be separated from her beloved daughter was very hard for her. But at least now she could send the money she earned for Kasia's support and know that she would not be in need. Of course this could not replace a mother's love. It was not easy for either of them, and Frania cried often at night, although she was by nature a calm, serene woman. She was planning to be reunited with her daughter one day in Kolomyja. Mama had promised to help her do so. I think that Frania transferred part of her maternal love to me. Kasia was two years older than me.

What Frania was now doing was truly courageous. Although she was not giving me any documents, just the fact of allowing me to use her daughter's name exposed them both to great danger. She passed me a bundle of things she had carefully prepared.

"Here, I have sewn some jewellery into the band of this wide skirt. These are the items that your mother gave me to take care of. Wedding rings, two other rings, a gold chain, and some dollars. That is everything that I managed to gather. And here are some of the German occupation *zloty* that you should hide in your bosom. You can use them both for your expenses. I still have your father's gold pocket watch. It is too big to sew in your skirt, so I think it's too dangerous for you to take it now. Perhaps one day I'll have an opportunity to return it to your mother. Now, listen carefully. Mama should stay where she is. I don't think she could find better shelter. Anyway, she shouldn't come back here. And you should volunteer to go and work in Germany. I know that some Jewish girls have carried it off. You look right, your Polish is good. They probably won't make too much fuss about the proper papers if you offer yourself as a volunteer."

"Probably..." "Too much fuss..." Easy to say, but could I manage it? How much danger was hidden behind those two phrases? Daring plans like that did not seem so easy to carry through. But I also knew that I could not stay here any longer. Both women, especially Frania, had already done far more than we could ever have expected. People had been betrayed and killed for far less money than Frania had already given me. She could just as easily have kept the money for herself – just as so many people had already done, people far better off and supposedly far more trustworthy. That much was obvious, but deep inside I was still bitterly disappointed that she hadn't mentioned even the possibility that she might be able to hide Mama and me in the flat. It was to be more than fifty years before I learned the very good reason why that was not an option.

It was my last night in Paulina's hospitable hut. Next morning, early, wearing the wrap, with the bundle in my hand, and bearing the blessings of both women, I headed back to Mama. I walked for the last time through the streets of my town. Here I knew every step, I always knew what was around the next corner. There were several ways to get to the railway station, but Frania ordered me to take the shortest. She herself followed some paces behind to make sure that I got safely to the train. But I needed so badly to have one last look at my family's home. Despite everything Frania was doing for us, I felt great despair that she would not even let me look in that direction. I wanted so much to spend a little time within its friendly walls, even if I had to stay locked in the pantry cupboard. Why did she keep insisting that none of the family could ever show themselves there?

I came to a decision. Whatever the consequences I had to walk past our flat and past my school too. I headed that way, squinting behind me. Frania started signalling frantically to me, but I pretended not to see and carried on. Although it was early morning, the streets were busy. Peasant women wearing wraps like mine were hurrying to the marketplace carrying milk cans and egg baskets. Around their shoulders they wore the characteristic *hucul* double bags made of *wareta*, a homemade fabric of woven coloured strips. One bag hung in front and the other at the back, so the burden was distributed evenly and the hands were left free.

Men in caps and simply dressed housewives mingled with the peasant women. Here and there, a lady wearing a hat and with a maid following behind, went on her early shopping round. The hated German *Feldgrau* (field gray) uniforms had not appeared thus far. It would be much later in the day that they would march through the streets, singing "Heili, Heila, Heilo" and arrogantly wasting time.

Now I had come to the town centre. There was our home, and I passed right under

Leap for Life

the balcony, near the windows of what had been our shop. They were not shining the way they used to. Instead of the colourful and varied delicatessen and fruit, all that was sitting in the shop windows were some sad, dust-covered bottles of vinegar, and pictures of food. I furtively wiped away a tear. Frania, who was still following me, shook her head in disapproval. I hurried up. I could miss my train because of this sentimentality. I was almost running. How wonderful that Frania had already bought me my ticket, which I had carefully hidden in my bosom the day before with the money. There was the station, with the clock showing I was there in time! It was still twenty minutes before the train was due to leave.

The windows of what had been our shop and the balcony above

The platform was crowded. When the train arrived the wave of people boarding carried me with it. Of course it was impossible to get a seat in the crowded carriages. I was just happy to get a place in the corridor near a window, which did not even have any glass in it.

There was Frania on the platform! She caught sight of me and I waved to her. The train started to move and gathered speed. Frania, with her hand lifted in a goodbye gesture, got smaller and smaller. I could not see her any more. Suddenly I felt terribly lonely in the crowd. What would happen to me? Did I have any future?

Everyone stowed their bundles and somehow made some room for themselves. I myself knelt on my bundle. From the next compartment echoed the sound of someone playing a harmonica. I could hear talking and laughing. A bottle of home-brewed vodka passed from hand to hand. And a friendly hand appeared in front of me offering a bright red apple. I sank my teeth into it. The juice dribbled down my chin. Not even the best fruit from our shop had been as sweet as this apple now tasted. Despite war and in contrast to it, people still could be friendly to each other. Could this really be true?

Suddenly there was a commotion. People were yelling, 'grab the little Kike.' Somewhere at the end of the corridor I heard roars and the fairy tale ended. Again I was surrounded by the horrible reality, but for now it was not me they were after, but somebody else. A little boy just like me. Boys, of course, are more difficult to hide. People around discovered that he was a Jew. They surrounded him and handed him over.

It is doubtful if the hunters knew about the Nuremberg laws of 1935, but they certainly knew how to live by those laws. They did not allow us for a moment to forget that we were people outside the law and that anybody could hunt us like animals.

The monotonous clicking of the wheels slowed down. In spite of my horrible situation I dozed off. For the young, that is the way nature is. Eventually people started to stir and I woke up. We were nearly there. The passengers prepared to get out. So, after almost three hours, I found myself back at Stanislawow station.

Chapter 3

Last Goodbye

This time I had to wait only an hour to change for the train back to Bukaczowce. That was good. I would arrive in daylight. I would stay overnight with our kind friends and the next day I would set out to join Mama. I was sure that Mama was in contact with our friends.

Those were the thoughts going through my head on that last stage of the journey. But when I got to Bukaczowce, I sensed immediately that something was wrong. The little town, usually so alive, was now strangely quiet. When I reached the square I saw that the windows of the Jewish houses were boarded over and their doors double locked. I could not see any trace of people with the Star of David armbands, although not long ago, when I left, there had been so many. The now silent houses had been full of life. My heart sank with a sense of terrible foreboding. Had there been another 'action' here? I had to find out what had happened, but I had to do it very carefully.

Suddenly I heard the sound of church bells. I had forgotten that today was Sunday. I had an idea! I could go to the church. I knew that women liked to gossip in the churchyard after the service. I was right. The churchyard was humming like a beehive. And everybody was talking about Friday's 'action'. From bits of overheard conversation I managed to put together the terrible picture of what had happened.

Not long after I had left, the Ukrainians and the SS had surrounded the Jewish quarter. They went from house to house with pedantic German thoroughness and Ukrainian cruelty, evicting the people and combing each building for any who tried to hide. Those who resisted were shot on the spot. The streets ran with blood. Those who were left were herded into a square near the railway station, where they were kept for a day and a night without food or water. Women, old people, children. On the morning of the second day they had been forced into cattle trucks and taken off into the unknown. Except it was not really unknown where they were going. The same well rehearsed script was being followed. The methodical German machine had not failed. The little town was proclaimed *Judenrein*.

The estate at which Mama had found shelter was a few kilometres beyond the town. How could I contact her without endangering both of us? The short autumn day was already coming to an end. I tightened the wrap more closely around me and

Last Goodbye

started off in the direction of the estate. I had walked only a short distance when dusk fell. In a field nearby were hayricks. I went over, burrowed a hole in one of them, and crawled in, carefully covering the opening. I ate the last of the bread given me by Frania but I hoarded the little milk left in the bottle. I would need it for tomorrow. I settled down to hide until the morning.

On the estate, Zosia's day – for that was the name that Mama had taken – would start very early. She had a lot to do, mainly in the kitchen, since she had now turned into a very good cook. Where had she learned this skill? At home she never had time to do anything in the kitchen. The meals she cooked were just what her *Treuhander* boss liked, so he was well pleased with her.

The estate was medium sized, and before the war had belonged to a family that was well regarded in the area. They had taken care to keep it in good condition. An avenue of linden trees led to a typical Polish manor house with columns at the main entrance. Behind the house there were solid brick buildings which housed the poor relations, referred to as 'residents' and where the steward also lived with his family. Each day two dozen people sat down at the 'master's' table, so the kitchen had to be large and well equipped. Everyone sat according to his status, and from portraits on the walls bearded Polish noblemen wearing robes and swords, and their women dressed in Polish cloaks and huge skirts, looked down on their descendants.

At the time of the outbreak of war in 1939, the family consisted of a couple known as 'the older masters', their only son, his wife, and their two daughters. The men were immediately called up, since they were both reserve officers. After the defeat of September 1939, they had probably both fallen into Soviet hands, because no one knew what had become of them. Meanwhile, their property had been confiscated from the women and only by a miracle had they avoided being deported to Siberia. In the first few days of the Soviet occupation they had managed to get through the still unstable border to the German occupied, so called General Government area, so they had spent two years in exile in Warsaw. They had managed to save some of their jewellery in the chaos, and that was what they had lived on.

When, in July 1941, the tide of history turned yet again and the Soviets were driven out of Poland, the Germans tried to woo back these Polish gentry, telling them that their estates would be returned. So the two women came back with the children. But of course, the occupiers, just as so many times before, had no intention of keeping their promises. The family found that they had to stay in the outlying buildings, since the *Treuhander* was lording it in the manor house itself. The institution of *Treuhander*, which literally means 'steward leader' came into being after the Germans realised that the Polish gentry, even after their bad experiences with the 'Reds', would

35

Leap for Life

not collaborate with them. On the contrary. In fact this, the most patriotic sector of Polish society, provided the core of the resistance to the Nazis.

The *Treuhanders* claimed roots as *Volksdeutche*, which means Polish people of German origin, but often they were merely Germans, moved to Poland into the newly conquered territories. Their job was to take charge of the economy. But, above all, they were to detect and stamp out any political activity by uppity Poles. Unfortunately this was a task at which they often succeeded, causing many arrests and much repression.

Indeed 'Zosia' had found her job with one such *Treuhander*, who came from the Poznan area. There was a constant coming and going of high ranking German officers from the *Wehrmacht* and *Gestapo*. They expected to find good hospitality and to be well lubricated with alcohol. So it was very important to have a good cook.

Just as the *Treuhander* could not tell the difference between the Polish Galician nobility and their Ukrainian servants, so it was easy to persuade him that Mama was just an ordinary maid. But Pani Maria, the older sister, immediately realized that something did not make sense. She suspected that Zosia could not be the person she claimed to be. So Mama thought up a new story, designed to be easier for her to believe. She explained that she really came from Lwow, but that she had had to flee because she had been involved in an Underground plot. She had been unmasked and had to change her identity, but had no papers

While the officers in the manor house were holding noisy celebrations of the early victories in the east, the Poles in the outbuildings were quietly going about private business of their own. Some so-called 'cousins' arrived, dressed in riding breeches and knee high boots, and some 'girl friends' of Pani Miodsza, the younger sister. They did not stay long, but it was enough to arouse suspicions in the main house.

Mama overheard the Germans planning an *action* in the outer buildings. They had no idea she could understand what they were saying – indeed how could a lowly servant like her have acquired such knowledge. She tipped off Pani Maria, thereby gaining both her confidence and gratitude. To have such an informant and ally seemed like a very good idea to Pani Maria and she decided to make a deal with Mama.

"I could try to get some papers for you. But you would have to keep an eye open for our interests in the big house, just like you're doing now. We are in debt to you because you told us what the Germans were going to do and we were able to cover our tracks just in time. Thanks to you they found nothing, so we hope we have lulled their suspicions for the moment. The papers would be false, of course. I have connections with the right people, and will try to get good ones. But you will have to pay well for them."

Last Goodbye

Mama was very happy to agree. It was no guarantee of safety, but it improved her chances. She would have opportunities to resist the Germans, and maybe in the future of making connections with the Polish Underground. Mama did not know if Pani Maria believed everything she was telling her, but it certainly looked as if she believed that Mama had been involved in some kind of plot.

All this had happened in the short but eventful time when I had been in Kolomyja. Mama had learned immediately about the Friday *action*. Tragic news travels only too fast. She had been worrying about me very much. How would I cope? Every day she went to the road several times, looking for me. And so it happened that in the early morning after my sojourn in the hayrick, we ran into each other's arms. We had succeeded. In the face of so much danger we were together again. But for how much longer? Although death still threatened us from every side, we were now in a much better situation. We had the jewellery and some money, and, in spite of everything, we had new allies.

Pani Maria was expecting Zosia's daughter to appear with money and information. And then Zosia's daughter would return to Lwow, where her aunt lived. Pani Maria suggested to Mama that I could stay for few days. But of course she did not know that there was no aunt, no home, and no return to Lwow for me. It would be better if the *Treuhander* did not know about my staying, Pani Maria suggested. My mother agreed wholeheartedly.

Mama told me everything when we met on the road. In return I told her what had happened in Kolomyja. And also about Frania's idea that I should present myself as a volunteer to work in Germany.

"I must think about it. This is a very tricky and uncertain business," she answered hesitantly.

Immediately after September 1939, alluring posters had appeared in occupied Poland recruiting volunteers to the Third Reich. They promised easy work, good wages, and comfortable living. Perhaps at the beginning they succeeded in fooling a few simple people, but now, by the end of 1942, nobody believed such promises. People knew that what would await them would be hard slave labour, and often cold and hunger.

In the Reich itself, there were now ever fewer workers. The men were fighting on the fronts with which the Reich was now surrounded. In Germany only women, old men and children remained. They could not manage the hard work that Hitler's war machine needed. So the Germans carried off from all of conquered Europe *Zwangsarbeiter*. As the name, forced workers, shows, they were far from volunteers.

In Poland these modern-day slaves were obtained by levies imposed by the occupiers. Each parish, village or town had to hand over a certain quota. Of course people defended themselves against this enslavement in various ways. When the Germans realised that the levies were working inadequately, they started to organise *razzias*, round-ups. They would set up a cordon surrounding a few busy streets, a railway station, or a market place. Those who were able to work they pushed into waiting trucks and they were shipped to transit camps. From there, after a rough *selection*, they were taken to forced labour camps in Germany. Older and middle aged men and women often fell victim to such round-ups, but above all they took the young. If anyone looked strong and healthy, they did not ask how old he was. They even took fourteen year olds.

Anyway, by this time it was very rare for anyone actually to volunteer to work in Germany. To do so would draw suspicion not only from the clerks who administered the system, but from the people who were to share the misery of slave labour. It was here that Mama foresaw the greatest danger. She would have far preferred to keep me with her. But this was impossible. If we were to have any chance of surviving, we had to separate from each other.

Meanwhile she led me to Pani Maria, who with her daughter-in-law and her two children occupied a four room flat with a spacious kitchen in the outer building. Considering that this was wartime, their situation was not that bad. They had a good supply of food, the rooms were well furnished, and now that the first frosts of autumn had come, there was heat in the large tiled stoves.

But what made me happiest were the books. In the room which was to be my temporary shelter, the shelves were filled from floor to ceiling with books! There was also a large desk, a sofa with fancifully carved feet, a table and four matching chairs. When it turned out that this was the room in which I was to sleep, I felt blessed.

Books! They had been ever-present in our house, and had been with me from earliest childhood. This was not because of our parents. No, Mama never did any reading, she did not have time for such things, and perhaps no interest either. Father read the newspaper regularly, but he rarely reached for a book. That changed a little in the 'Russian time,' when he had nothing to do. But even then he did not read novels, rather he turned to nonfiction.

It was my older brothers Salek and Pawel who brought in books, and who read them avidly. Pawel who was then in high school did not have much to do with a little girl like me. So it was Salek who led me into the magic world of fairy tales. He read to me the wonderful stories of the Grimm brothers. Some people say they are cruel, but they did not seem so to me. Then, when I grew older he led me to the books of Kipling, Makuszynski and May.

Last Goodbye

I remember vividly how much I longed for the time that I could read for myself. Because I was so impatient, I got the knack of reading very early, and indeed nobody knew how I did it. I remember only that the first things I read were the shop signs. At that time there were very many such signs, and they were all different, not like today. Above every shop was a large painted sign on which you could read in big letters the name of the shopkeeper and the business the shop conducted. Some of the signs carried simple, but colourful illustrations. I would walk along the streets with my head turned upwards, reading them out syllable by syllable. After that I learned very quickly. I started to read everything that I got my hands on, everything that my brothers brought home from the library. Sometimes the books were not at all suitable for a little girl.

Salek tried to guide my greedy, chaotic reading. He made efforts to suggest worthwhile books. In history, Polish patriotic history, he led me through Sienkiewicz and Kraszewski. In poetry through Mickiewicz, Slowacki and Pawlikowska. He himself, passionately and in secret, wrote romantic poems for which I was the first and perhaps the only audience. During this time close bonds grew between us, and he became for me an authority who could never be undermined. I admired and loved that older brother of mine, and tried to be like him. I could always bother him with my childish problems and he would treat them seriously and objectively. Later on, when I was at school, the teacher wondered how I had read so much, and attempted to steer my zeal.

In the ghetto hunger for books gnawed at me no less than real hunger, although the latter was of course more tangible and painful. To be honest, I even succeeded in smuggling into the ghetto (without my parents knowing) in my personal rucksack two or three books – I remember that one of them was Zeromski's *Syzyfowe Prace* and I read them over and over so many times that even today I can recite the story of Marcinek Borowicz by heart.

Pani Maria shook her head with a knowing wink, seeing how tenderly I was stroking the spines of the books.

"Be careful, child, and don't forget that you are meant to be the daughter of the nearly illiterate Zosia."

The week I spent in the friendly home of Pani Maria I remember as the most peaceful period of the war. Bathed and well fed, I could spend all the time I wanted drawing from the library and indulging my passion.

Mama, when she could, but not too often in order not to awake suspicion in the *Treuhander*, slipped to the outer building and whispered and conspired with Pani Maria. The result of all of this was the arrival of the papers, including a baptismal certificate in which it was written in black and white that Zofija Baranczuk was of Ukrainian origin and had been baptized in the Greek Orthodox church. Now the *Treuhander* could register Mama on these terms.

We sighed with relief. At any rate Mama was safe for a time. Now, she only had to stay hidden and be careful that no one recognized her, though achieving this would be as easy as balancing on a narrow wire above a chasm. But what about me? Pani Maria knew only that I was living with my aunt in Lwow, and that I had come from there to give Mama money to buy false papers. She knew also that Mama came from an educated family and was hiding after a failed plot. And that was the way it was to stay. She had promised that I could remain for a week. After that I had to go home. And only Mama and I knew that there was no home and no aunt.

Somewhat reassured by Mama's situation, I decided to persuade her to let me try to go to Germany by applying at the recruiting point in Tlumacz. Mama was against the idea, and thought of thousands of problems. I tried to put her mind at ease as far as possible.

"You see, so far nothing bad has happened to me. I have managed to learn my part. I am sure I will be fine. Anyway, we have no other choice."

Eventually I succeeded and the decision was made. The day after tomorrow I would go to Tlumacz. Pani Maria and her daughter-in-law Janina gave me a hearty farewell. They invited me to come back 'after the war'. My God! After the war, three words which meant so much, some mythical country of constant happiness and justice! But would we live to see it?

I left in the early morning, well supplied with food for the journey. Carrying my few belongings tied in a bundle, and with my ski boots on my feet, I was marching out to conquer Germany and to save my life. Mama insisted on going some of the way with me. We would grab the chance to spend a few more moments together.

We kept silent. Mama was crying noiselessly. There she was, having to surrender her youngest, smallest child as prey to be hunted in the cruel world. What was awaiting her? Would she survive? Why couldn't she protect her child from the dangers threatening from every side? Had she nursed her just to surrender her into this, the cruellest of all wars? Questions and doubts to which there could be no answer. But she had simply no alternative.

How could any mother stand such heartbreak? But she had to. She was the Jewish mother of the time of the Shoah. The most courageous, the most devoted. She would do anything to give her child a chance, the chance to survive.

We were near to the hayricks where I had spent the night. Mama had to go back. We hugged each other tightly. I tried to keep my face calm. I wanted to let out a great howl of despair. At last I pulled myself from her arms and ran. At the bend in the road I turned back one last time. She was standing in the middle of the road with her hand raised in a gesture. Was it goodbye or was it a blessing?

That is the way she remains forever in my memory.

Chapter 4

Away To Germany!

It was getting close to the end of 1942. I found myself in Tlumacz shortly before noon the same day. I decided to act immediately. In any case, I had already burned all my bridges. There was nowhere else to go if I failed, so I just had to carry it off. Determinedly, I approached the first person I saw after leaving the railway station and asked where the *Arbeitsamt*, or work administration office, was. It was not far.

I was soon standing in front of an imposing building. I went in and found myself in a long corridor with many doors, each bearing a nameplate. Ah! 'Department of Work In Germany'. This was it. I knocked and opened the door without waiting for an invitation. The woman sitting behind the desk looked up questioningly.

"Good morning. I would like to offer myself for work in Germany."

Yes?!!" The overwhelming astonishment in her voice made me lose my self confidence.

"And how old are you? "

"Sixteen, and I will be seventeen in January," in an instant adding two years to my age. "You see, it's like this." Now I was stumbling and improvising, blundering in deeper and deeper.

"I am an orphan and until now I have lived with my aunt in Tarnopol. But things are very bad there. My aunt has several small children of her own, her husband hasn't come back from the war, and she has made me feel again and again that I am a burden to her. So I have decided to run away and offer myself for work in Germany. I'm grown up already. At my aunt's I am often cold and hungry, and she's always hitting me. So I thought it couldn't be any worse in Germany."

I looked at her hopefully, pretending to be a bit simple. The woman got up and came round from behind her desk. "Now I'm finished," was all I could think.

"Sit down there and wait, I'll be right back."

She pointed me to a chair. When she left I fell into a panic. Surely she had seen through me and was going to come back with a policeman. What should I do? Run away? But there was no time and to do that would be to admit my guilt. "You only live once, you can only die once." I recalled the saying of the Cossack in Sienkiewicz's

Away to Germany!

trilogy. From now on it would be my motto. So I sat down on the chair as if I hadn't a care in the world, although inside I was trembling with fear. In a short while the woman came back, followed by a man.

"So you are from Tarnopol?" he asked, "What is going on there now? I come from there myself."

How I blessed those quiet talks between Frania and Paulina that I had been part of. I had never been in Tarnopol. But Frania had talked so vividly that I could guide myelf around the town quite well in my mind.

"Oh really! Perhaps you know my aunt? She lives on Mickiewicz Street, you know, near the church? The one which was destroyed by the bomb in 1939. But don't give me away. I don't want to go back to her. I want to go to Germany."

"Why did you decide to come here, to Tlumacz?"

"I came with a friend who has family here, and she wanted to volunteer with me, but they told her not to. I was afraid that they would tell me to go back to my aunt." I stammered on like one possessed, trying to silence the fear deep inside me.

"Well do you have papers."

"No, how could I? I told you, I ran away. I left my birth certificate there."

He went to the woman at the desk, and the two of them whispered together.

"So," he said, "the lady will write down your personal details and will give you a document which you can present at the assembly point."

Personal details! Documents! I could hardly believe my ears. Wonderful! I would have a document that stated in black and white that I was Katarzyna Raduga, the daughter of Franciszka, and so on and so forth! Could it really be so easy?

Indeed it was. The woman rolled a form into the typewriter, asking me questions and typing the answers. It took her a long time because she was not a skilled typist. When she had finished, she showed me where I had to sign. I did so in big scrawling letters, careful not to betray myself by appearing too skilled. Unexpectedly, and to my huge disappointment, she did not hand the document to me, but called a guard and, giving him 'my' papers said,

"Please take her to the assembly point, and bring back this person..." and here she rummaged in her desk and took out a form like mine.

"Ah!" I thought. "That's why they've agreed so quickly. They're using me to rescue someone else and balance the numbers. It looks as though I've been lucky rather than clever." The guard took both documents. I rose, pulling my wrap tightly around me, and holding my bundle. I was ready to go.

"So, I wish you luck." The woman smiled at me. Fear gripped my throat again. Could she have guessed something?

Leap for Life

We headed into the street. He walked quickly, holding my hand. Perhaps he thought I would run away. But I was not even thinking about it. Rather I felt that I was walking on air. Mama! I had to let her know. She was surely sick with worry. She would be so happy to hear.

"Please, Sir," I pulled on the guard's sleeve, "can I buy something in this kiosk. Where I am going it will not be possible, will it?" He nodded agreement. "But be quick and don't try any tricks."

I untied some coins from my handkerchief. "Please give me a postcard and a stamp, and an indelible pencil." Luckily they had what I needed. Particularly the indelible pencil. At that time they were used instead of pen and ink. You only had to moisten the black lead. Such writing could not be erased, unlike the case with ordinary pencils. and it had a nice violet color.

We entered what turned out to be a fire station. People of all ages, guarded by armed Ukrainians, were sitting or lying on straw pallets ranged around the walls of a huge room. Approaching one of the Ukrainians, my guard handed him both documents, and explained something, pointing at me.

"*Tycho* (silence), he shouted. Suddenly the loud buzzing of conversation stopped. All eyes turned towards us. He called out a name. A young fair-haired townswoman went up to him quickly. The Ukrainian verified her identify card and nodded his head.

"Yes, it is OK. You can leave with the guard."

In this simple way I exchanged places with the fair-haired woman. We were both happy. She because she was able to leave. I because I now had proof of my new identity, and could stay.

I crouched down on the straw mattress indicated to me. The people around me went back to their interrupted conversations and their own business. They were not very cheerful. What would happen to them? They faced an insecure future far away in Germany, in an unknown and enemy country, as virtual slaves.

The group gathered in the room represented a cross-section of the society of the area. You could tell at a glance who came from where. There were those dressed more or less prosperously, but in a way that identified them as townspeople, and who spoke Polish. They were the victims of round-ups and often had only what they were wearing. Some had battered suitcases with their poor belongings. These by some miracle had been delivered to them by their families.

But most of the people came from the countryside. They spoke Rusinski, a Ukrainian dialect from the Carpathian Mountains or *Huculszczyzna*. They had gathered together in groups, local people from the same villages, predominately poor illiterate peasants now torn from their roots, bullied and intimidated. One such group occupied the corner near me. It was mostly women and they came from a village somewhere near Jaremcze. They had with them large wooden cases containing clothes and food. Presumably they were victims of the levies. One of them, a fat, large-bosomed woman who was wearing a gathered skirt and a short, sleeveless sheepskin, stroked my hair.

"Such a *detyna* (child)! Come here *doniu (*sweet daughter), would you like to join us?"

I willingly accepted the invitation. I preferred to be with the simple peasant women rather than with the town 'ladies'. It was easier to blend in with their background. My lack of Ukrainian and anything different about me would be put down to my being Polish. Of course in this group I could not admit that I was a volunteer. I remembered all too well Mama's worries. So, on the spot, I thought up another story about an orphan and the wicked aunt, who had handed me over to Germany in place of her own daughter. So they gave me their sympathy, and Jekaterina, because that was the name of my new friend, decided to take care of me and mother me a little.

Dusk came. I was extraordinarily tired from the constant tension. All day I had had nothing to eat, and I had hardly thought about eating. Now that things were a little more relaxed, I took some food from my stores. Some Pani Maria had given me. The rest Mama had got hold of somehow from the *Treuhander*'s kitchen. People around me were settling down to sleep, lying in their clothes on the straw pallets. I used the rest of the daylight to scribble a note to my mother on the postcard I had bought. We had arranged that if everything went well I would write to Frania saying that I had got home safely and that my aunt was well and sent her greetings. Frania would be the go-between for our correspondence and would forward messages on to Mama. I hoped that I would have a chance to post the card the next day.

I lay down, with my little bundle under my head, and covering myself with the wrap, tried to fall asleep. The talk around me became quieter and quieter and soon I could hear snoring. I tossed around on the straw pallet, and images from my unbelievable and exhausting day kept going round and round in my brain. My head was spinning from thinking up so many new versions of my life. My eyes were burning from tears I dare not shed. But in the end my tiredness overcame me. I fell into a deep sleep. It was my first sleep for many, many days that would not be haunted by horror and nightmares.

A lot happened in the week after I volunteered for the labour draft. First we were brought from Tlumacz to Lwow, where we waited for several days until there were enough people to fill a transport. At the transit camp we were required to surrender all our possessions for disinfection – even the clothes that we were wearing. After being issued with a piece of grey soap, we were herded into a huge shower room with nozzles high on the ceiling. Suddenly water poured onto the crowd, first scalding and then freezing. After a few minutes of this entertainment, the guards turned off the water without caring whether we had had time to soap ourselves and to rinse. Of course, we could not dream of such a luxury as a towel.

Then, still naked – obviously another Nazi method of humiliation – we were lined up for a medical examination. A few in German uniforms and a few Polish doctors made the medical decision about whether we were fit to work. We were called up by name from the papers we had had to surrender and which were piled on their desks. I happened to be called to a Polish doctor. He looked critically at my undeveloped body, still without pubic hair, and said: "Hmm, my child, it says here that you are sixteen, but you do not look it. I think I could arrange for you to be released and sent home, but a German doctor would have to approve this."

"No, Doctor, please don't do that," I cried out in panic. Then I looked around in case someone from my group had heard. Luckily, I could not see anyone I knew. "You know, doctor, I am a volunteer," I said very quietly to the doctor. He looked at me, questioningly, and a flash of apparent understanding crossed his face. "Aha, so we will let you go, if you want to so badly. In any case, I will write in your papers that you are a volunteer. Maybe they will treat you better." Before I had the chance to stop him, he wrote, in a slanted hand, on the margin of my priceless document, the word *freiwillig* and handed it to me with a knowing smile. I was aware that although he had had the best intentions, he had done me a bad turn. It was important that no one should know that I was a volunteer, particularly my new friends, the Ukrainian women, since I had told them something very different. So, I had to think what to do. It was exhausting keeping all my stories straight and not letting in any contradictions. But I had to, if I was to survive.

They kept us waiting a long time for our clothes. Shivering and humiliated in our nakedness, we huddled together like sheep trying get a little warmth and to protect ourselves against the brazen stares of the uniformed males. We got them back eventually, crumpled beyond recognition and stinking of disinfectant. But the number of lice had not dwindled. On the contrary, ideology notwithstanding, their races had been mixed together and invigorated. We spent a few more days in this transit camp, which was not far from the rail yard where the wagons were assembled for the transport to the *Reich*. As usual with the Germans, the organisation was perfect.

And then I was on a moving train again. The monotonous clicking of the wheels and the swaying of the carriage made me drowsy. Compared to that other, nightmarish train, this one was luxurious, although it too was a cattle transport. There was enough space to move and each wagon had several bundles of straw. We got fed. So why was that earlier train always in my mind? Why did I hear that screaming all the time?

It was getting colder. And the lice continued to torment us. It was now the third day of the journey. We did not know where they were taking us. We did not know what our fate would be. Since we had crossed into Germany, they stopped watching us, and did not even bother to bar the doors to the wagons. We did not know the language and we looked very different from the local German inhabitants. Now and again the train would stop in open fields, or outside a station, to let through trains carrying soldiers and supplies for the Eastern front. On the station walls we could see banners with slogans, *Raeder mussen rollen fur den Sieg* – Keep the wheels rolling for victory. From time to time they would push some loaves of coarse dark bread into the wagons for us to divide up among ourselves, and occasionally a military kitchen with stacks of metal bowls would pull up and give us hot soup.

We were disgruntled and unhappy. The worst was the uncertainty. There were rumours that we would be used in huge war factories, and that the conditions there were appalling. In any case, the people I was with had been hoping to work on German farms – *Bauer*. This was because most of them came from the country. I was frightened too. I would not fit in on a farm. In fact, I would not fit in anywhere, since I had hardly worked at all in my life. Jekaterina tried to comfort me. She said,
"Don't worry, just stick with me. With me you will survive, I am strong and I know how to do the work. I will help you, and in return you can write letters for me, because I do not know how to write." I accepted the bargain happily. But would they allow us to stay together?

Another of the problems on the trip was meeting our bodily needs. We tried to do so when the train stopped. But we could not go far from the train because we never knew when it would start moving again. So we had to keep our eyes open and overcome our modesty. By the time the train moved on, the area where it had stopped neither looked nor smelt good. And it was worse when someone had to 'go' when the train was moving. He or she had to do so in a corner of the wagon, in front of everybody. I had become quite a different person from before. What had happened to the well bred girl?

I lost track of time. But it must have been the end of November 1942 when at last we reached a large city. At the station I read the name Metz, which I did not know. They led us through the grey dawn, along clean paved streets. The oncoming trams were almost empty. I followed my old habit of reading all the signs, and some of the

Leap for Life

names seemed strangely French. Could we be in France? No, that would be rather unlikely.

They led us into a red brick barracks, surrounded by a tall fence. It turned out to be another transit camp. People from all over occupied Europe were waiting here for assignment to different workgroups. The rumour mill was working hard, still producing contradictory messages in every one of the many languages gathered together in this contemporary Tower of Babel. After the next, now-routine, delousing, we were divided into smaller groups. Each group had to wear a different emblem. I got a red apple on coloured paper. So did Jekaterina and a few other women from the same village. Maybe this meant that we would stay together? I overheard someone say that Metz had belonged before 1939 to France and that it was the capital of Lorraine.

All this time I had been wondering how to get rid of the incriminating word *freiwillig* from my document. At last I had an idea, a very simple idea, to tear off the corner on which the word was written. On such a long trip, during which papers had been examined so many times, it could easily have happened by accident, and would not arouse suspicion. Secretly, I performed the operation, and breathed a sigh of relief. I was still very frightened all the time, although I could not admit it, even to myself. But behind my plucky mask hid a terrified little girl who had no one to whom she could turn for safety. Yet in spite of all this, I was happy that I was succeeding. Maybe I would survive in this huge unknown Germany? Maybe Mama would survive too? Maybe this war would not last too long and we would be reunited, never to part again.

That is what I pretended to myself. I pretended that I did not know that such happy endings only happened in fairy tales.

Chapter 5

The Shoe Factory

Another train. Now, because we 'apples' were a small group, we travelled in a normal passenger train, but segregated in separate compartments from German travellers. After a few hours, we reached our destination. It was a small town, or rather a village, with only one platform. A few local inhabitants also got out of the train. They passed us indifferently, jabbering among themselves. Obviously we were not an unusual sight.

The guards led us through the village. Ahead was an enclosed area, surrounded by a fence topped with barbed wire and with a big iron gate. Above the gate, mounted in an iron semi-circle, was the name *Rovo A.G. Schuhfabrik Speyer* – the Rovo Shoe Factory of Speyer – written in stylised lettering. So, I thought to myself, not so bad, it is only a shoe factory. I was careful not to reveal that I could read and understand it. What I knew, I kept to myself. So my old German lessons had finally come in useful. I had not liked the *fraulein* who had taught us German, but Mama had insisted that we learn it.

The iron gate closed behind us with a harsh sound. We found ourselves in the factory yard. Only women, about thirty of us. In front of us stood a German in his brown SA uniform in the standard overbearing pose. I had learned to recognize this uniform long before in the Kolomyja ghetto, because being able to recognize it often meant the difference between life and death. Standing next to him was a young woman who obviously, from the way she was dressed, was not a German.

The SA man, in a commanding voice, made a speech in German. The young woman was meant to translate for us. But she translated into Russian, which. although similar to Ukrainian, could not be understood by the Ukrainian peasant women. Since they knew that I been to Russian-speaking schools during the period of Russian occupation, it was safe to let them know that I understood what was being said. Whispering, I tried to explain to the women standing near to me what was going on. The Herr Direktor was telling us that he expected us to work willingly and productively for the Third Reich in general and for the factory under him in particular. And if we were not willing to do so, he would get the considerable help of the Gestapo to teach us. So we

49

were not to try any sabotage. Most of us did not even know the word. But during his speech, he repeated the word again and again. If he had intended to intimidate us, he succeeded very well.

"You will live here." Nadia, our interpreter, led us into a big room with narrow bunks. Opposite was a washroom with cold running water. The toilets were in a tiny building outside. In the middle of the main room stood a big table, and on it an iron pot, with steaming soup in it and a pile of steel bowls and a stack of spoons. The cook, a fat German woman in a spotlessly clean white apron was ladling out the steaming liquid. One by one we went up and she gave us a bowl of soup and a slice of black bread. There were no chairs, so we sat on the side of the bunks to eat our first meal in our new quarters. The soup consisted of water, yellow foul-smelling turnips and a very occasional piece of potato.

"Lights out is 8 pm, wake up is 4 am, and you must be at your machines by 5. Tomorrow morning I will take you to the factory floor and you will be assigned to your particular supervisor and jobs. The Russian girls from my group who have been here a long time will instruct you. You will learn it. It is not difficult." So spoke Nadia.

Thus started our work in the small village factory, a branch of a large company based in Speyer. The Russian girls had been working in the main factory in Speyer, and had now been moved here to teach us what to do.

Life was difficult. There was little food, not enough to live on, but too much for us to die quickly of starvation. The work itself was not very hard. I was assigned to the sewing machine room which was above the ground floor. Compared to the large, cold, and very noisy downstairs production room, this was much more pleasant. It was almost warm, indeed it was much warmer than our dormitory. We worked twelve hours a day, with a short break for the main noon meal, actually the same inevitable turnip soup. For breakfast and supper we got bitter black *ersatz* coffee and a slice of bread.

Christmas and New Year were approaching quickly. Just the thought made my friends tearful and sad. How would they spend those holidays – normally so full of family and friends – now far distant from their villages and traditions, and locked away almost in a prison. Up to this point they had not let us even stick our noses outside the iron gates. I cried too, although from quite other reasons. But at least when everyone else was sad, I did not need to hide my own grief.

In daily life I carefully matched my every action to the Gentile world around me. Like everyone else I knelt each evening by my bed of wooden planks and prayed. Like everyone else I told stories about home and about how Christmas had been, about

The Shoe Factory

how we used to go to midnight mass and about the carols we would sing. Thanks to Frania and Paulina and our old neighbours I knew a lot about these things. But all the same, sometimes I would make mistakes. Fortunately only I seemed to notice them, but even so, those mistakes caused me a lot of fear and anxiety. I worried that others would notice them, and come to their own conclusions. But it never happened. My work mates seemed to have enough problems of their own, and probably believed my stories – or so I told myself as I veered between optimism and depression.

Almost every night I would dream of our home, about my brothers and my parents, and about Frania. Sometimes the dreams were happy, but more often they were nightmares. When I woke it was hard coming to terms with the awful reality of the present. I was always scared that I would give myself away by my moans and screams in the night.

* * *

Our house on Pilsudski street had been built in the days of the Austro-Hungarian occupation. On the top floor, where the kitchen and nursery were, there was a characteristic balcony running along the whole building at the back. From it you could walk straight into our rooms through a French window. In later years I was to see similar balconies in the old neighbourhoods of Vienna, Budapest, Prague and Krakow.

At one end lived a Polish family called Kowalski. The father was a widower with a large number of daughters – possibly up to seven girls. I remember Jozia, the eldest, but best of all I remember Jancia, who though only four years older than me, was effectively playing the role of mother to her sisters. The father terrified me. A gloomy and bad-tempered looking man, he found it very hard to feed all his little ones. But the daughters, particularly Jancia and I understood each other very well.

Jozia helped to support the family by doing piece work at home for the Kolomyja curtain factory. Jancia often helped her, working on the balcony, embroidering the fabric with flowers or geometric designs before the curtains were finished at the factory. They looked very attractive hanging in the windows of the town. But the work was hard and not very well paid. We would sit out on the balcony together while the needles sped back and forth in Jozia's and Jancia's skilled hands and chattered about everything vital to us. I could never get enough of this talk, and thanks to them I learned a lot about life, about the real world and its problems and dangers – something that at that point I knew little about.

When Christmas came, Mama would prepare a large box full of delicacies and fruits, and there were also some clothes for the girls. Usually it was my job to deliver the box to our neighbours' home and put it under the Christmas tree. Despite their modest circumstances, the tree was there every year. It went without saying that I would spend Christmas Eve with them, sharing the evening's treats, following the old Polish custom of breaking wafers and exchanging good wishes, and enjoying a hearty meal of traditional Polish Christmas Eve dishes, all cooked in advance by Jancia. Officially, of course, I should not have done that because the food was not kosher, but my parents did not enforce the rules very rigorously.

Once, in great secrecy and without telling the grown-ups, Jancia took me with her to her Church. It was an unforgettable experience. I was terribly frightened because I was disobeying not only my God but also that other God whom Jancia worshipped, and I was convinced that I would be severely punished right there on the spot. I held Jancia's hand tightly in my own sweating one, peering suspiciously around.

"Don't be afraid, silly, just do what everyone else does," Jancia encouraged me quietly. So I knelt and rose together with everyone else. Jancia had already subjected me to a special course in crossing myself before we came to church! When I realised that I was not about to be struck by a thunderbolt from above, I started to look discreetly around me. I liked it.

It was even more beautiful than our Great Synagogue which, in fact, I did not visit very often either. When, during the Assumption, the silver voice of the little bells was heard, with every head bent low praying, and this was then followed first by dead silence and then by the whole church echoing with the music of the organ and the singing of the congregation, I thought to myself, if there is a heaven, this is what it must be like.

* * *

Those earlier friendships now repaid me with my life. They made it far easier to pretend, and to avoid mistakes or false moves. But I still had to watch every movement and every word. It was difficult, and I paid a heavy price in nervousness and fear.

My fellow workers belonged to the Greek Orthodox Church which celebrates Christmas a few days later than the Roman Catholic one. But since we had only two days off work, starting on December 24th, that was when we all celebrated together.

These were sad holidays. Yes, the German officials did allow some of the women into the kitchen to prepare traditional *pierogis* instead of the turnip soup, and yes, that night, for the first time in a long time, we did more or less eat our fill, but every moment of our supposed treat was bathed in tears. We cried at our current situation, and in fear for our loved ones; we yearned for our homeland and longed for our

The Shoe Factory

freedom and for the view and air of the Carpathian Mountains. And I had so much more to cry for. Now, when I no longer needed to hide my tears, I let them flow endlessly. I could think only of all my loved ones who were gone. Surely for ever. But no. There was Mama. There was Salek in Russia. Maybe they would survive. But what was happening to Salek now? Was he wandering, starving and freezing, homeless and lonely in the endless depths of Russia? On his own, deprived of home, family and friends? And why had this happened to us? What terrible sins had we and our ancestors committed to bring down such cruel punishment on us?

One of the women started to sing a carol. Everyone else joined in. These simple uneducated women harmonised wonderfully. Their melody, usually sung at midnight mass inside the small Orthodox churches of their little villages, now carried far into the cold winter night, into a strange and unfriendly sky. We stayed up late that night, singing and remembering.

One day shortly after Christmas, Nadia brought in a bundle of marked envelopes with one piece of paper in each one. She announced that according to German war regulations we were allowed to send home one letter every six weeks. I had long been wondering how I could let my mother know that I was alive and relatively safe, so I was delighted. We all were.

I set to work with my indelible pencil. Because I knew how to write, I took dictation from those who were illiterate. So I had plenty to do. Nadia had told us that the letters would be censored, and that if there was something in them that the Germans did not like there might be trouble, either for the writer or for her family at home. So it was clear to me that I had to choose my words so that one could read between the lines whatever could not be said openly. Moreover, when I came to write my own letter, the style must not seem different from that of everyone else. So I began "in the name of the Father and of the Son," and ended up with greetings to all my 'relatives' and to half the 'village' population, exactly as my friends had asked me to write to their families. When I came to address the envelope, I faced another problem. I could not send the letter to Mama at the *Treuhander*'s, because that would set up a direct connection between the two of us, a line that could be traced by anyone hunting us. In fact, I did not even have the address written down, because Mama felt that it would be better if there were no written record.

So I decided to send the letter to Frania, just as I had sent the postcard while on the way here. She knew Mama's address and would be able to find a way to get my news to her. In addition, since I was using her surname, it would be obvious that Frania was a relative of mine. I told the other women that I was writing to a cousin. They knew that I was an orphan, and that I would not be writing to my 'evil' aunt.

Leap for Life

About six weeks later, replies started to trickle in. Every now and again one of us would get a letter from home. Each was a great event. The letter was first read to the recipient, and then, with her agreement, to the whole group. They all came from the same village where everyone knew each other well. I alone was a stranger, but since I was writing and reading their letters, I came to be seen as more like one of them. They came to trust and accept me.

At last my day came. "Katarzyna Raduga," announced Nadia loudly. It was her job to distribute the letters which a postman had delivered to the factory office. "It's for me," I shouted with joy. Already I could recognize Mama's bold handwriting. "Thank God she is alive," I thought as my shaking hands tore at the envelope. "That's from my cousin, I will read it to you later," I told the women who were watching me.

The news was not so good. Mama had done a wonderful job of adopting my code and was using Frania as a contact point; the letter had Frania's return address. I learned that Mama was well, that she was still working at the same place, but that : *"at Aunt Maria's place everybody, even Maria's guest, has caught an infectious disease and is now in hospital. I am still healthy, but I am afraid that I might also catch this disease, because I took care of them. I should move to a place with a better climate, but I do not have the money. I received your postcard which you sent during your travels. I am glad that you are doing well in Germany."*

It was not hard to read this obvious code. I concluded that something had gone badly wrong at Pani Maria's and that Mama was somehow involved. "That's not good," I thought, "that could be the end." I hoped that soon I would be able to send a second letter. Maybe things would be cleared up by then. I was very anxious.

The days passed, monotonous and without hope, each day like the one before. We did not even know how the war was going. Then one Sunday we were permitted to attend the village church. It was the first time we had been allowed outside the factory gate. We looked very different from the local inhabitants. We had not had much chance to wash our clothes, let alone to iron them. Cold water and the tightly rationed soap were not enough to keep things clean.

But there was among us one group of women, the daughters of more prosperous farmers, who had brought with them in their wooden suitcases their brightly coloured Hucul folk costumes: ankle-length embroidered linen tunics, gathered panels at front and back, bright red high laced boots, and embroidered sheepskin coats. So far they had not had any opportunity to show them off. Now they decided to get dressed up for church. When Nadia saw them, she was full of admiration.

"Wait, we will make a show for the Germans." She begged one of the girls to lend

The Shoe Factory

her a costume. Nadia was quite a beauty even without dressing up, and so she looked a real picture in the outfit. With Nadia and the brightly dressed group in front, we set off for our first walk in the village.

As we left the church, standing under a big lime tree, we were surrounded by German women and children. They liked the girls in the folk costumes. But suddenly they noticed the rest of us, grey and emaciated and wrapped in rags. They started talking together and some of them disappeared, coming back shortly with plates full of slices of their traditional Sunday cake, which they offered to us. We all started to eat and some of the Ukrainian women tried to be friendly and to start a conversation.

But not me. I did not believe in their kindness. On the contrary, I just could not understand how it could be that these women, who were not without human impulses, could be the wives, daughters and mothers of those blood-thirsty monsters whom I had encountered in the streets of the ghetto during the *razzias*. Did they know that their men would split the heads of infants against concrete walls? Did they know what their beloved *Führer* was leading them to? But those were questions that I could only ask in my own mind, and which no one there could answer.

The spring of 1943 was coming. Cut off from the press, the radio, and even rumours, which might have been a source of rising hope, we did not know what was going on at the battle-front. But of one thing we were certain, bombs were now falling on German cities. More than once we had heard the noise of explosions and had seen the glow of fires above the nearest city, Speyer. One day the bombs even fell on our village. Although they did not do much harm, they had a huge impact on me.

On that day the machine where I usually worked was broken, so I was assigned to another job. I was to iron leggings. This was done with a heavy iron at a very thick wooden table. Suddenly we heard first the air raid warning sirens and then the sound of planes and the explosions of bombs. The Germans left the factory in a hurry heading for the concrete shelter. We were told to go back to our dormitory. The air raid lasted a long time and after the sirens sounded the all clear we did not go back to work, since it was late at night. The next morning, the first thing I saw when I entered the sewing room was a group of Germans surrounding the place I had been working the day before, with the *Direktor* in front.

"That's her. She was working here yesterday," one of the men shouted when he caught sight of me. I did not know what was going on, but I could tell that something was wrong. When they moved back, I got a sight of the table. There was a hole in the shape of the iron in the thick top. God! In the chaos of yesterday, I had forgotten to turn off the iron. What would happen to me now?

The *Direktor*, red in the face, shouted about sabotage, the security police, the

Gestapo. He grabbed me by the hand and pulled me towards his office. Nadia was called and the investigation started. I could understand what they were saying and knew that I was in great danger. Fortunately, the boss of the sewing room, my supervisor, was there. She was a kind middle-aged woman, and took my part.

"What sabotage, Herr Direktor? Look at her. She is still a child. She hardly knows what the word sabotage means, or how to count to ten. Probably she forgot to turn off the iron because she was scared of the bombs." She tried to minimise it. The Herr Direktor softened a little.

"You are lucky that there was no fire. If that had happened, you would not have escaped the concentration camp," he told me through Nadia, who was no less scared than me. "But I do not want you here any longer. You will be taken back straight away to the forced labour centre in Speyer. They can decide what to do with you."

I went to the dormitory for my pitiful belongings. They did not even allow me to say goodbye to the other women. A new sense of terror engulfed me. And just as I had been naively thinking that I would be able to survive the whole war quietly in this factory.

Guarded by one of the factory officials, I was delivered by local train to the *Arbeitsamt* in Speyer. For the first time I walked through the streets of a real German city. Although I was still fearful about my future, I looked with the joy of an avenger at the many ruins caused by the air raids. There were hardly any men to be seen, but there were many women, young and old. Some of them were in the uniforms of the Wehrmacht auxiliary services. Everyone in civilian clothes was wearing a turban-like head-dress made from a scarf, as the latest wartime fashion. How different I looked, wrapped in my grey-white checkered shawl, my wide skirt, and my ski-boots, the only thing I had that reminded me of the time before the war. Inside those boots were still hidden what was to me my greatest treasure, the three little family photographs that Frania had given me when I left Kolomyja, the last relics of my lost world.

* * *

In January of 1939 my parents had bought me a ski outfit that those boots were part of. To the south of our city there was a mountain which, at least to my youthful eyes, was quite high. It was called Oskrzesinska, after the village at its foot. What memories we had of that mountain! It was where my brothers and their friends went hiking in the summer. Sometimes they also took me with them. The trip usually took two days. We had to go along the Prut valley, staying overnight in one of the Hucul barns, sleeping in fresh smelling hay. There were rustlings, and sometimes a mouse, but what did that matter on such a splendid adventure! In the morning of the second day, we would take a ferry across the Prut, because the only bridge from Kolomyja was far away in the opposite direction.

The ferry was a boat with a flat bottom and sides. We crossed into it by a narrow, shaky gangplank. Apart from the passengers, it carried wooden chicken coops full of cackling poultry. Sometimes there would also be a pitifully bleating lamb or a pig squealing at full throttle, and tied up by a string around the leg. The ferryman would collect the fares, then set his Noah's Ark moving off towards the opposite bank. The ferry would be rolling and my heart would be in my mouth for fear that we would sink in the fast flowing Prut. But, sitting between my brothers Pawel and Salek, I did not reveal my fears. I knew that if I gave myself away, they would not bring such a coward along the next time. I put my best face on it, so that the boys would not know how scared I was.

In the winter we would go skiing there. The bells on the horse's neck would ring joyfully as we raced in the sled across the frozen Prut and through the pure white crackling snow. Later we would rush from the sleigh and Salek would teach me to ski. At the beginning I would constantly fall over, but then I got the knack of it. What joy and laughter there was! In the winter twilight we would return home and Frania would be waiting for us with a cup of hot tea and, still warm from the oven, that wonderful sweet cinnamon doughnut we called *Buchta*.

Could the world ever really have been like that?

Chapter 6

The Maidservant Katrin

Once again I was marching in my heavy ski boots from the days 'before' and still the three precious pictures were stuck under the inner sole. These boots were indestructible – my parents had wisely bought them two sizes too big, and now they were in stark contrast to the rest of my terrible outfit. Many in the street looked at me with pity or contempt. I felt helpless and humiliated.

On the way to the Arbeitsamt, I tried to prepare myself for whatever would happen there. Surely they would know about my supposed 'sabotage' at the shoe factory, surely there would be an interrogation and punishment. As so often in my wanderings things went very differently from what I had feared. They did not ask any questions or conduct the threatened investigation into what had happened at the factory. They just added me to a large group of men and women of various nationalities. As well as Poles and Ukrainians, there were Czechs, Serbs and French people. We were led back to the station and put into a specially separated carriage on a passenger train. I heaved a sigh of relief. Maybe I could carry it off yet again.

It was many hours before the train arrived at our destination. It was nighttime. They uncoupled our carriage and shunted it onto a siding together with its cargo. Then, early in the morning, a woman clerk appeared carrying our papers. Shortly after, one by one, German peasants started arriving at this slave market. They looked us over, evaluating our potential as labour for their farms.

Apparently nobody wanted me. I was small, and emaciated from the hunger of the shoe factory. They must have all come the same conclusion, that I was not suited to farm work. Well, they were right. I really had no idea of what it would involve. Nor indeed, of what any job would involve. As the only and long awaited daughter, I had been cosseted by all the family, and so was totally unprepared for hard work.

Suddenly a man appeared and started to explain something to one of the clerks, who turned to us and asked, "Does anyone speak German?" This was my chance. I made a split-second decision. Now, after being here for a few months, I could safely admit that I had learned a little of their language.

"*Ich, nix viel*", I answered in a deliberately foreign accent of an *'Auslander'*.

The Maidservant Katrin

(Me, not a lot).

The clerk signalled me to follow the man she had been speaking to. He led me through the streets of a city that had been untouched by war. The occasional passer-by still carried a hint of elegance. I listened carefully; their language did not sound German. I realised with astonishment that they were probably speaking French. Was I really in France, I asked myself. We approached the city centre. From the market square radiated little streets of gable-roofed, green-shuttered houses. We passed small shops with gleaming windows. Even though there were not many goods, they were something I had not seen for a long time. On some of the houses the metal shutters had been opened and the gentle breeze caused the snow-white curtains to billow out through the open windows. Here and there women appeared carrying brooms and buckets filled with water which they poured over the pavements in front of their houses and scrubbed them clean, shouting a friendly 'good morning' to each other in their musical native language. Although it was only the beginning of March, you could feel spring in the air. Buds were bursting on the trees and the borders were filled with colourful flowers. The town was silent, peaceful and full of harmony. Was it really possible that elsewhere in the world war was raging, and hate-filled people were killing each other with great cruelty.

We were just passing a shop which had paintings in its windows. My guide directed me to its entrance. The bell attached to the door announced our arrival in the shop and an elegantly dressed woman appeared through the curtain which separated the shop from the house.

"I brought you the housemaid you asked for," announced the man who had brought me. He noticed that the woman was looking at me disapprovingly." She speaks German, as you wanted. There was no one else who could." In some anxiety he tried to talk up the goods he was offering.

"Really?" She turned directly to me. I nodded. I sensed that she was warming a little, but that she still did not like the look of me.

"*Has du Lause?* (Do you have lice?)" she asked, touching my shawl with disgust.

"Yes, I do," I answered almost happily, hoping that it would perhaps tilt the scales against me and that she would send me away. I did not like her either and I did not want to be a housemaid. But to my amazement, my words had the opposite effect. Maybe she liked my honesty, or perhaps her need for a German speaking housemaid was so desperate that she nodded her head with resignation. "Very well, since she is already here, let's keep her. But we have to get rid of the lice." The man clicked his heels and departed.

"*Komm mit* (Follow me)". She led me through a concrete yard to the laundry at the

Leap for Life

back. She ordered me to throw down my wrap on the concrete floor, and to light a fire under a copper boiler filled with water, and then to take off all my clothes. Nervously I watched her pick up all my precious belongings with iron tongs and throw them into the fire. The flames devoured everything – even my bundle. "*Nein, Schuhe nicht* (No, not the shoes)," I shouted in panic when she was about to throw in all I had left from home, not so much scared for the boots, as for the pictures hidden inside them.

"Why ever not?" She looked at me with astonishment, then examined them carefully. At last she said, "Perhaps you are right. They really are good quality. Genuine leather. How did you get such boots?"

The question might have been innocent, but I was terrified. My fear of being unmasked, my constant companion for so long, reared its head again. I did not answer. I had not yet prepared a new story. But the woman did not press me. She put on a pair of rubber gloves and with two snips of a pair of scissors she cut off my braids. They followed the rest into the fire.

"Pour some hot water from the boiler in here and take a thorough bath." She pointed to a tin tub, handed me a piece of household soap and left.

I sank with relief into the hot water. What would happen next? Would she give me something to wear? Oh, what's the point, I shouldn't worry about it, I told myself. I soaped my body and my hair thoroughly and scrubbed myself with a stiff brush. I could feel the dirt peeling off in flakes. The water became grey and filthy, but there was more in the boiler, clean and hot. So I emptied out the dirty water onto the concrete and refilled the tub. The whole laundry grew warm and steamy. I felt that I was as light as a feather and that all my troubles were melting away in the clouds of steam. I closed my eyes and found myself back at home.

Another of those 'boot pictures' was of me and a schoolfriend dressed up in Hucul folk costume just before war broke out.

* * *

The Maidservant Katrin

Our house in Kolomyja was quite old and had only partial plumbing. Our weekly baths were taken in the kitchen, in a tin tub that was stored in the pantry. On the kitchen stove we would heat a large kettle of water. I would sit in the bath, smelling of pine cones and good soap, and Mama would wash me with a soft sponge. A warm, fluffy towel was waiting in which Mama would wrap me from head to toe. On the kitchen table a tasty supper would be waiting. It would usually be a cup of cocoa or Ovaltine, with slices of raisin bread. Salek would carry me piggy-back, warm and sleepy after my bath, to my clean soft bed in the nursery. "Read me something," I used to beg.

* * *

Without warning the door opened. Immediately I pulled myself together. "My" German woman stepped into the laundry, carrying an armful of clothes and a bottle in the other hand. She threw me a rough towel. "Dry yourself properly, and then bend your head over," she ordered. She poured a nasty smelling liquid from the bottle over my head and told me to cover my hair with a piece of white linen. She carefully checked that not one stray strand of hair peeked out. When she treated my boots with the same liquid I was so thankful that my precious photographs were hidden and safely wrapped in waxed paper. She gave me my new clothes. They were a bit shabby and a size too big, but they were clean and in one piece. I got dressed, first underwear, then blouse. I had to hold the skirt up at the waist with a piece of string. For my feet I got worn down shoes. My new mistress looked me up and down critically. "Well, at least we can let you in the house now! Clean up here and then come upstairs."

I did as she had instructed and left the laundry. There was an ironwork spiral staircase leading directly up from the yard. On the next floor were two doors, one on each side of the landing. After a moment's hesitation I opened one of them to find myself inside a big, bright kitchen filled with the delicious smell of food. Goodness, was I hungry!

The mistress was busying herself in the kitchen. A cup of hot *ersatz* coffee with milk appeared on the table and next to it a plate with slices of bread, thinly smeared with sugarbeet jam.

"Sit down and eat," she ordered. She did not have to repeat herself. I threw myself upon the food, biting off big chunks of bread and burning my tongue with the hot coffee.

"Well, your name is..." here she looked through the papers that my guide had given her, "Katarzyna Raduga," she pronounced with some difficulty. "That's enough to tie your tongue in knots. What did they call you at home? Kasia? No, that is also too difficult. I will call you Katrin," she decided.

Leap for Life

    I nodded my head and kept quiet, for my mouth was still full of the food which was rapidly disappearing while the *Frau* kept talking.

    "My name is Alfrieda Grossman. There are five in our family, myself, my husband Paul, our fifteen year old son Helmut, eleven year old Hilda, and Hans, who is fifteen months old. I am sure you have noticed that I run a shop which sells original paintings, so I do not have time to deal with the housework. Now that will be your job, and you must begin immediately. Start with the dishes and the kitchen. Then I will show you the rest of the house and explain what you have to do."

    She was using short fragmented sentences, as if she still did not believe that I understood German. I did not disabuse her. On the contrary, in my answers I tried to adopt her way of speaking, while also letting her know that I understood what she was saying. She left. Next to the sink was a piled up mountain of dishes. It looked as if no one had washed up for a week!

    But the kitchen was splendid. I had never seen anything like it. It was tiled from floor to ceiling. The floor tiles also matched the overall decoration. Near to the coal burning stove there was also a gas stove, with coloured knobs, four burners, and a baking oven. At home we also had a gas stove, but it had only two burners, and no oven. Our kitchen had a white and blue tiled frieze with pictures of Dutch windmills and girls wearing large clogs, but it only went around the stove. We had a marble washstand but no running water, no sink, and certainly no shining brass taps. So I did not know how to use them.

    Eventually, I turned the one with the letter W on it for *Warme,* meaning hot. In a device above the sink something crackled and crashed and suddenly a blue flickering appeared. Hot water ran from the pipe. What a marvel! I shook my head in wonder and started to wash up. It took me a long time, since I was inexperienced and there was such a pile of dishes. I managed to finish them but I realised I was not going to have an easy time of it.

    The ancient four storey building was narrow, and was one of a row of similar houses. On the ground floor was the shop, the yard, and the laundry with the cellars beneath. Then came the kitchen, the living room and the dining room. Above them were the bedrooms of my masters and the younger children, a guest room and the bathroom, which was splendid. It had a big, white, enamelled bathtub, with shining golden taps, and mirrors from floor to ceiling. On the top floor, there were only two rooms. The first, larger one belonged to the son of the house. But the little one – what a miracle – turned out to be for me. My own separate world. Actually, I did not get much chance to make use of it, for my free time was limited to a few short hours of the night. But having my own room gave me a feeling of privacy that I had longed for for many months.

The Maidservant Katrin

At first the job was more than either my strength or my skill could handle. "Frau Frieda," for that was what my new employer wanted me to call her, was not really a bad woman. She explained things patiently and showed me how to do everything. At the beginning I was very slow, but as time went by I became more experienced and managed better. In spite of this, because the workload grew, I could still never catch up. My day started at 4:30 in the morning and did not end till around midnight. But worst of all was laundry day. Then I had to get up even earlier.

I would go down to the laundry where the washing had been put to soak the day before. I would light the fire under the copper to heat the water and then stand for hour after hour by the washtub, rubbing the washing against the tin washboard. Although I used all my strength, and though my knuckles got bloody from the rubbing, the washing seemed never to get any cleaner. Worst of all was wringing out the large items. It was only then that I came to appreciate fully Paulina's hard work and her skill. And Paulina was a strong adult woman who was used to it. I was a 15 year-old underfed girl.

To my astonishment, the day after my arrival, when the Frau was sure that I was free of all the lice, I found myself seated with the rest of the family at the dining room table. Compared to the shoe factory, the food was delicious, but I had been so underfed for so long that I never felt really satisfied. Although we ate together, the worst and the smallest helpings always ended up on my plate. I tried to find a bit extra in the kitchen, mainly from the leftovers, but I did not get much opportunity because the food pantry was kept locked.

Slowly I started to work out the overall situation. The small town was in Alsace, the province that prior to 1939 had been part of France, but that even earlier, like our own Silesia, had changed hands several times. Between Germany and France, it had been a continuing bone of contention. The local population used both languages. I was not able to judge their French since I recognized only the rhythm of the language, and their German was an awful dialect barely understood even by native-speaking Germans. But the locals were always very nice to me. When I was sometimes sent on an errand to a small shop, they would often press something into my hands, a bread roll or some sweets. Once I even got some real silk stockings, the first I had ever had, of which I was very proud.

The Frau tried to complete my wardrobe, probably with cast-offs from the patrons of her shop. So, one after another, I gained three changes of underwear, two blouses and skirts of a more suitable size than the first ones, shoes, and a quite nice green coat. I also slowly gained weight, developing a few curves, changing from a skinny teenager to quite a pretty girl. My plentiful hair was by now properly cut, and looked neat, my complexion was healthy, and my eyes shone. Once a month, on Sunday, I got time off to go to church. Although I still looked poor, I did not really look very different from the general population, and quite a few young soldiers would turn their heads and try to get my attention.

I liked the Sunday outings. They were the only change from the constant grey and the continuing slavery. At least, here in church, I could sit down in peace without the continual "Katrin this" or "Katrin that." The people of Alsace were mainly Catholic, and on Sundays many of them attended the late service. But the early mass attracted only a small congregation so it was easy for me to explore this new and unknown world.

With the sensitivity of youth, I absorbed the impressive spectacle of the Holy Mass. The ritual gestures of the priest, dressed in his richly embroidered vestments; the baroque interior of the church with its holy pictures and sculptures of bible scenes; the solemn sound of the bells carrying into the clean, still morning air; the silver sound of the little bells announcing the consecration, and the silence that followed. I could not hold back my tears, which I let flow freely down my cheeks. In my mind I was seeing those near and dear to me. The women sitting nearby looked at me with approval and apparent understanding. They thought I was deep in the emotion of prayer.

During the first days that I was at this new place, I had sent a letter addressed to Frania that was intended for Mama. But weeks passed and I got no answer. I was scared that the worst might have happened so far away. During the night I cried my eyes out into the pillow and had many nightmares. Although as far as I knew I had thoroughly covered my tracks, and was almost sure that nobody would see in the forced worker the Jewish girl inside, I still never for a moment lost the feeling of being a hunted and surrounded animal.

I got on very differently with the various members of the household. Since I was now speaking only German, I could allow myself to show increasing proficiency without arousing any suspicion, and the Frau was astonished at how talented I was and at how fast I was absorbing their language. Hilda was a nice girl, and little Hans was a sweet infant. I could not hate them, although perhaps I should have

With the lord of the house and his son, it was quite another matter. I always felt that they created a kind of terrible atmosphere which surrounded them. I came to understand this instinctive revulsion when I first saw them in uniform on what was probably a Nazi Party holiday. The father flaunted an SA uniform, and the son was in Hitler Youth garb.

Later I learned that they were both sworn Fascists. The father was very proud of the fact that he had belonged to the Party since its very founding. He had taken part in

The Maidservant Katrin

the so-called *Saalschlacht* during the famous meeting in the Munich *Hofbrauhaus*; he had been part of the Koburg street battle between the Nazi squads and the Communists and Socialists. My Herr had received a medal for this, of which he was very proud. During meals he often talked about those 'days of Koburg' and indeed, that was how I learned about them. The son proudly looked up to his father, the hero of the legendary events that had led to Hitler's ascent to power.

I never learned why the Herr was not fighting someone on the many fronts of the Reich, like so many other German men. What I knew for certain was that he held a cushy post at the local wine bottling enterprise, and that many benefits flowed from the job. His own cellar was very well supplied. The shelves were filled with bottles of splendid, well aged vintages. The middle of the cellar was dominated by two huge barrels of young wine, one filled with white, and the other red. You only had to turn the tap and wine poured out in a stream. Among my many other jobs, it was my duty each day to fill a jug from each of the barrels and deliver it to the table

The Herr came originally from Bavaria and liked to draw attention to that fact. In the summer he would wear *lederhosen*. There was always a long stemmed pipe hanging from his mouth. I do not know how bright he was – I certainly never saw him with a book, although there was in the living room a large glass fronted bookcase containing many books. *Mein Kampf*, covered in black leather had a prominent place. But he surely knew how to assemble multi-barrelled Bavarian oaths like *Kreutzhimmeldonerrweter.*

It was from these books that I really learned to master the language. When I was cleaning the living room in the early morning hours while all the rest of the household was asleep, I just could not resist trying to penetrate their secrets. How astonished I was to discover – after spelling out the titles with some difficulty – dear familiar friends, among others Kipling, May, and my beloved Brothers Grimm. Naturally, I could not resist the temptation, now and again, to reach up and borrow one of those books and hide it in my room. Later, when I could at last get to bed, I would try to read a page or two. I rarely got far because I was so tired, and would often fall asleep after reading only a few words.

One day this caused an uproar. I had an alarm clock in my room which would wake me before dawn to start work, since I had to be the first up in the house. I do not know if, on this ill-fated day, I forgot to set the clock, or if I just did not hear the alarm. At six in the morning, surprised not to hear me busy at my tasks, Frau Frieda took it upon herself to check what was going on. She came into my room to find me sound asleep, and worst of all, she found an open book on the floor by the bed. It had probably slipped down when I fell asleep.

Leap for Life

The outburst went sky high. How dare I, a Slavic 'lesser person' reach for the high treasures of German Culture? I got my first severe beating from Herr Paul. And he knew how to beat methodically with German thoroughness and with the skill of an SA man. He used a broad leather belt. For many days I could not go out for my face was all bruised. But my owners did not allow me to take time off to recover. I had to do all my work, even though every part of my body ached, and I could hardly move. Of course I was forbidden ever again to make use of the bookcase under threat of even more severe punishment. But it was of no use. I just became much more careful.

By the beginning of 1943, the Germans led by General Paulus had already suffered their terrible defeat at Stalingrad. But they were still enjoying significant victories on other fronts, particularly in the Caucasus. Often, when I was busy in the living room, I would hear on the radio the announcement that *Oberkommando der Wehrmacht gibt bekannt* (the Military High Command has an announcement), after which there would be fanfares and the pompous voice on the radio would list victories and give the names of conquered cities. The family celebrated every such occasion by drinking a bottle of vintage wine. Their toasts were *"Heil Hitler"* and *"Fur denn Sieg"* (To Victory). And my heart bled.

But strangely, even though I was then only an under-educated and inexperienced girl, I never doubted for a minute which side would have the final victory. I believed absolutely that the Nazis would lose this terrible war that they themselves had unleashed, and that it was only a question of time. But time was for me the ultimate enemy. This was a race. A race in which millions of lives were at stake.

A few days after the fuss about the book, at last the long awaited letter came. "It's for you," announced Frau Frieda, handing me an envelope that had once been white, but which now, covered with numerous notes, crossings out and stamps, looked more like a scrap of dirty paper. It had been addressed to the shoe factory, but that had been crossed out, and in its place was written my current address, confirmed by the stamp of the Work Administration in Speyer. I turned the envelope over cautiously in my hands, not daring to open it under the watchful eyes of Frau Frieda. It seemed to me that she was watching me even more carefully than usual.

The handwriting was completely unknown to me. In a split second, a hundred thoughts rushed through my mind. Among others that, once again, this confirmed German thoroughness, that I had not covered my tracks as I had thought until now, that somewhere in their files my every step had been carefully noted, and they knew exactly where I was at this very moment. I hid the envelope in the pocket of my apron.

"It's from a friend of mine, who thinks I am still working in the factory. I will read it later," I said, trying hard to look unconcerned.

The Maidservant Katrin

It stayed there all day, and thoughts of it weighed on my heart like a heavy stone. I did all my tasks like an automaton, until the time in the late evening when I at last found myself in my room. With trembling fingers I tore open the envelope and took a quick look at the date, it was from three months ago, and at the signature. It was signed "Frania" but it was not in Frania's handwriting. All these facts I registered in a split second, while at the same time reading the short text.

Dear Kasia

Your beloved Aunt Zosia has by now surely written to you about the epidemic that broke out in Pani Maria's home. Sadly, your aunt who nursed them also got infected. The disease turned out to be fatal and all of them passed away.

I know how painful this is for you, but I have to let you know. As for you, please do not write any more. Not to my address, nor to Pani Maria's.

I wish you the strength to bear this blow. May our Lord Jesus Christ have you in his care.

Frania

In my head the hammers reverberated again. They banged faster and faster until once again I heard that screaming. The screaming of the tightly packed, naked bodies and the rhythmic sound of the train wheels. Then everything became quiet, and very far away, on the horizon, appeared Mama's silhouette, with her hand waving goodbye to me like a weeping willow twig moving in the wind. Then I slipped into unconsciousness.

When I came to, I was lying on the floor of my room, gripping in my hand that letter of unbearable suffering.

In the morning I had to pull myself together to do my work. Mama was dead, but I had to go on living. I knew this was what she would have wanted.

This was the day I was to have my photograph taken for my identity card.

I have the picture to this day. In it, my eyes speak great sadness.

Chapter 7

German Disasters

Life went on. I was still working very hard but my body was developing properly, and I was learning to work more efficiently. Although the food was not enough to stop me being forever hungry, little by little I continued to put on weight. But the period of acute hunger had left its mark. Boils appeared at various places on my body. I had to hide them. I knew that the Frau would not be happy if she found out about them, and that they could have unpleasant consequences for me. I was allowed to take a bath in the laundry, so, late in the evening, after finishing my work, I would set up hot baths for myself there. This caused the boils to burst. They drained and slowly started to heal, leaving behind only ugly purple scars..

At night I would cry. Even if I were to survive the war, probably there would be no one to return to. Sometimes I would hope. Maybe Salek at least would be able to survive in Russia's dangerous vastness? But even that glimmer of hope would fade quickly. I realised that surely the Germans would have caught him during that eventful summer of 1941. They had advanced so fast deep into Russia then. And he, like all our males, carried the mark...

During the day, I did not have time for such thoughts. I was cleaning, washing clothes, doing the dishes, carrying out and beating heavy carpets, washing windows, preparing ingredients for meals. I had to cope with these and countless other tasks in that luxurious, well appointed house. Frau Frieda did the cooking herself. Perhaps she did not trust my culinary abilities, or perhaps she was just afraid that I would grab a little more to eat.

My first job each morning was to wash the pavement in front of the shop and polish the shop window. One day, when I was cleaning the door frame I recognised a familiar diagonal shadow. A trace of a Jewish *mezuza*.

So that was the how it was. This house, and everything in it had once belonged to a Jewish family. Doubtless a well-off family. Now I understood where all those fine utensils, the dinner service, the pictures and the knick-knacks came from. Undoubtedly that family, like us, had had to leave their home with only what they had been able to carry. They had been forced to leave behind property collected

German Disasters

perhaps over generations. What had they been like, and what had happened to them now? Were they still alive? If so they were certain to be desperately homesick, and thinking back to what had once been their home, just like I was thinking back to my own. Perhaps their fate had been even worse than mine. I certainly knew about the forced deportations of Jews from places like this. About deportations to the East to concentration camps and extermination camps.

Again and again my mind went back to that letter of ill omen, trying to decipher it in various ways. It was absolutely clear to me that it had been written in code. The "sickness" of Pani Maria and her visitors I understood to mean that they had fallen into a Nazi trap. Everybody was aware of the methods the Gestapo used in their interrogations. What had probably happened was that someone had not been able to stand the torture, and had eventually betrayed the others, causing everyone else to be arrested. Perhaps they had all been executed. Very likely that was what had happened. But I could not be sure.

Maybe Frania knew the answer. But she had clearly given me to understand that she did not want me to write to her. Perhaps she was afraid that the links between us would be uncovered. In any case I should not put her in danger. Did Mama die because she gave information to Pani Maria's network, or because she was a Jew? Endless questions without answers. All I had were terrible suppositions and imagined scenes. Even if I were to survive, I would not have anyone to go back to. Maybe I would not even be able to find a grave to cry over.

The monotonous days filled with work, crept by, and stretched into weeks. The weeks extended into months. I still survived. Still nobody discovered who I really was. I now had an authentic identity card, even if the dates were false. It recorded that I was a Pole, *Statenloss*, or 'stateless', which probably meant that Poland no longer existed as a sovereign country, and was never intended to exist again. The Germans might be confident of this but I was certain that they were wrong. Only I was not so sure that I would be alive by that time. My new identity document and the passage of time did help me feel a little safer. But the fear of being unmasked was rooted deep in my subconscious. Often some innocent remark would be enough to bring that fear back to the surface with redoubled power. By this time I could not even console myself with the hope that had till now remained in my heart, the hope of going home, home to Mama, back to my homeland. Whenever I thought about it, I felt the blackness in my eyes and the hammering in my temples. So I ordered myself not to think about it, at least not deliberately. As month succeeded month and still no one discovered my true identity, I sometimes started to feel that even I did not know who I really was.

Leap for Life

In the early morning, after I had finished washing the pavement, I used to clean the living and dining room. At that point, everyone else in the house was still asleep, so it was the best time of the day for me. I was not being summoned all the time, so I was able to get through my chores methodically. I even sometimes managed to take a quick look – with my ears pricked in case anybody was moving upstairs – into the bookcase or at the headlines in the morning papers, which I had always to place near Herr Paul's chair.

Frau Frieda attached great importance to family and to the aesthetic appearance of the table. She would prepare plates with bread and butter and marmalade and for 8 o'clock breakfast I would brew the *Ersatz Kafee*, coffee substitute, and pour it into a tall porcelain jug which was kept warm with a cover. This was embroidered with something like *Morgenstund hat Gold im Mund*, 'the morning hours are the best, they are worth gold'. Everyone in the house had his regular place at the table, including little Hans on his high stool. I sat at the very end, near the kitchen, ready at any moment to run one of their errands.

The fanfares from the radio and the announcements from the High Command became rarer, and then stopped completely. Herr Paul would become bad tempered and gloomy after his morning reading of the newspapers. It was better to stay out of his way, and I was careful to do so. One morning in July I again saw Herr Paul lose his temper, although this time I was not the cause. He started to shout abuse, and I was told to leave the room. But I soon learned anyway why he was so angry. It was the announcement in the morning papers about the Allied landings in Sicily.

During the next couple of weeks events moved with the speed of an avalanche. When the news arrived that Mussolini had been arrested, that General Badoglio had seized power, and that he had signed an armistice with the Allies, dissolved the Fascist Party and declared war on Germany, Herr Paul's fury reached its peak. He made no effort to restrain his outbursts. He thundered against those *Scheiss Italianer*, Italian shits, cowards and traitors, who had not hesitated to stab their old allies in the back.

And indeed, soon afterwards Italian prisoners appeared in the town, dressed in grey-blue uniforms. They were kept in a large building on the outskirts. Every morning at dawn, as I washed the pavement, I would watch them being lead in columns to work. The Germans treated them very badly. The nights and the early mornings were cold, and the prisoners, used to the sunny climate of Italy and dressed in thin ragged uniforms, almost barefoot, and certainly hungry, dragged themselves to the day's hard labour. I do not know why the Italian incident stuck so clearly in my mind. Maybe it was because my masters made so much of it and discussed it so much. Or maybe it was because of things that happened later, and that touched me so directly.

German Disasters

Helmuth, like his father, was upset by the Italian 'betrayal'. He was a blonde handsome teenager, tall for his age. Of all the family, I disliked him the most, even more than Herr Paul. But at the same time I was intensely envious of him. For many reasons. He had his parents and family around him and he could attend school. He would also insolently brag about his membership of the *Herrenvolk,* the 'Men of the Race'. When I watched him march with his fellow Hitler Youth dressed up in their uniforms, singing the *Horst Wessel Lied (Heute ist unser Deutschland und Morgen die ganze Welt-* today we own Germany, tomorrow the whole world*),* it reminded me so much of the others, those in black uniforms emblazoned with skulls, who had driven us through the streets of our town along a path of no return. Such thinking made my head throb again with the drum beats. No, no, I would stop myself thinking about it.

Sometimes, when I cleaned Helmuth's room, I would snatch a glance at his schoolbooks, being especially fascinated by the complicated algebraic formulae, which I had once seen in my brothers' schoolbooks.

* * *

There had been a time when they would both go off to school every morning, dressed in their dark blue school uniforms. Salek's uniform had blue trim, because he was in middle school, and Pawel's was purple, showing that he was in high school. Each had, in the appropriate colour, a circle on his sleeve with the number of the school on it. Each was the proud possessor of a specially designed cap with a visor which completed the uniform.

I could not wait for the day when I too would go to the *Gymnasium.* The girls used to wear dark blue pleated skirts and blouses with a large sailor's collar. They had a blue collar for everyday wear and a white one for special days. But sadly, my education had stopped abruptly after the fourth year, and it was only because of my passion for reading that I knew a little more about the world than my friends. At this point, the schools were not co-educational. There were about five girls' schools in our town and each one had its own special colour for the school berets. From that, and from the colour of the circle on our sleeves, you could immediately tell who went to which school. We, the girls from the school named after the great Polish poet Adam Mickiewicz, used to wear dark blue berets. I really loved that school, and looked forward eagerly to every school day. I had a lot of friends there, and two were especially close. But like most children, I loved the holidays most of all.

That last holiday, in 1939, had been particularly varied. First Dad and I had gone together to the mountains. It was the first holiday that we had taken alone together.

Our holiday detination – the beautiful Prut Valley

Early in the morning we would run along a stream not far from the cottage we rented from a peasant family. Gasping and splashing each other we would wash ourselves in its ice-cold crystal clear water. After breakfasting on dark bread, home-made butter and eggs, we loaded our rucksacks for a full day's hiking. The slopes, covered with spruce trees and warmed by the summer sun, smelled almost bewitching. At noon we made camp, reaching into the rucksacks for our food. Here Dad was very different from the way he was at home. We had long, deep, honest talks, which revealed him in quite another light. I became very close to my father during that time, closer than I had ever been before. It was to be the last opportunity that we would have.

We returned home tanned and happy. Now it was time for Mama's holiday. She worked very hard, but once a year she allowed herself to go away for a water cure, usually to a spa called Krynica. This year was no different. Although there had been rumours about possible war, the truth was that nobody really believed that it was coming. This summer Mama planned to take Salek and me with her. This departure was not as simple as it had been with Dad. One rucksack was not enough! Our trip was preceded by long preparations, including shopping, visiting the dressmaker for discussions about what was in fashion this season, and countless other chores, and then packing the cases and the unavoidable anxiety before departure.

At last the day came. A horse-drawn cab had been ordered to take us to the station,

German Disasters

and it waited in front of our house. Mama, together with Dad who was seeing us off on the train, sat in the comfortable seats, and Salek and I sat on the narrow bench facing them. The cabby arranged the bags behind the back seats, sat in the driving seat, cracked his whip and set everything in motion. The cab had rubber tyres and moved silently and smoothly. You could hear only the loud clip-clop of the horse's hooves on the cobblestones.

The whole train journey, including changes in Lwow and Krakow, took a long time, so we were quite tired when we finally reached the pension in Krynica where Mama was always welcomed heartily as a regular guest by the owner and the staff.

Wonderful indeed were those, our last holidays together, although we did not realise it then. Mama enjoyed a complete contrast from her everyday life, dressing up, visiting the baths, wandering with her friends along the promenade and chatting. In the pump room she would sit down and have a leisurely drink of the local healing waters from a special jug with a spout, which had painted on it a little landscape and the inscription 'Souvenir from Krynica'.

Salek would go off with his own crowd of youngsters, but sometimes I would succeed in persuading him to take me with them to Park Mountain or to the mineral spring, *Bocianowka*. *Bocian* translates as 'stork' and the water was supposed to help women who were having difficulty getting pregnant. Although the mountain by then boasted an electric railway – quite a technical wonder in those days – we preferred to hike up through the wilds, avoiding the beaten path. Salek and his friends had quite an adventurous bent, and I was proud when I was allowed to be in their company. We had planned to stay to the end of August. But it was not to be.

One morning in late August we were awakened by air raid sirens. It was the first time that I heard their shrill sound. It turned out to be an anti-aircraft drill. The same day the newspapers brought the shocking news of the signing of the so-called Non-Aggression Pact between Germany and Russia. The newspaper boys who loudly shouted out "Warsaw Courier" or "Evening Express" had no difficulty selling out of their papers that day! Panic broke out. Everyone wanted to get back home at once. And so did Mama.

We packed like lightning. There was a huge crowd at the station. There was clatter, commotion, and long queues for tickets. There were lots of young men who gave off a whiff of alcohol. They had probably been called up. I watched all this with huge eyes and a heart tight with apprehension. Many experiences that day I would come to remember as the "first in my life". Later, they would become routine. Mama managed somehow, with Salek's help, to get onto the train. Then he passed first me, then the luggage, through the window, pulling himself at the last moment onto the steps of the carriage.

We reached home two days later. It was August 29, 1939.

* * *

Helmuth wanted very much to be an airman. He dreamed of being one during this war and of fighting *Fuhr Führer, Volk, und Vaterland*, for Führer, People, and Fatherland. He saw himself as a hero honoured with a *Ritterkreutz mit Schwerten*, Knights Cross with Swords. Most of all he wanted to be the pilot of a *Stuka* dive bomber, so he often practiced "nose dives" with his little brother Hans. The child loved the game and laughed loudly when Helmuth used him as a fighter plane, swinging him first high in the air near the ceiling and then down low by the floor.

One morning the trumpets blared again from the radio. The news was so good that Herr Paul personally went to the basement to get a bottle of old wine. Helmuth delightedly brought his mother up to date on what had happened. His idol, the pilot Colonel Otto Skorzenny and his commandos had rescued *Il Duce* from his prison in the mountain redoubt of *Gran Sassso*. "You know, Mother," he declared during the dinner with its toasts in honour of this great event, "now we have shown those cowardly Italians that for a real Fascist nothing is impossible, and that we would go to Hell itself if our *Führer* ordered us. I too will be like Otto, and before too long. Now those damned Italians will fall into line!"

The phone rang. It was Herr Paul's friends from the Party inviting him and his wife to a party to celebrate the liberation of *Il Duce*. They left me in charge of the children, who were already asleep, and I was busy clearing up the dining-room after supper. I was bending to pick up something when suddenly I felt a hand under my skirt. Taken by surprise, I was pushed to the floor. A drunk Helmuth, breathing heavily, lay on top of me, trying to tear my blouse away from my breasts. At first I was completely overwhelmed and bewildered. Was that overbearing, supposedly 'higher man,' who never noticed my existence except to give me orders, now fired up with alcohol and fantasies of himself as a hero somewhere in far away Italy, about to commit *Rassenschande*, 'race shame' ?

"No! Never! Don't even think about it." I gathered all my strength and started desperately to defend myself, trying to push his body off me. Finally I managed to free one of my hands and dug my fingernails into his face. Caught off guard, he relaxed his grip. Instantly, I was on my feet, and shouting hysterically that if he did not stop immediately and get himself under control, I would tell everything to his father, who would never forgive such disgrace. The result was that he calmed down

German Disasters

and slunk away to his room. The next morning he got up before anyone else and slipped away to school. When he got back he spun a story about how he had fallen playing football and scratched his face. I wondered what yarn he had told at school. But from that day on he never bothered me.

The Germans did not get their way. The release of Mussolini did not change the course of the Italian campaign. As before, every morning frozen and hungry Italian prisoners of war shuffled along to work. But in the hearts of millions of oppressed people hope was awakening that the defeat of the enemy was getting closer. On the radio there were no more fanfares, just information about the location of the front lines. And slowly the names of familiar towns started to be heard. Czerniowce, Stanislawow and Lwow. So by now Kolomyja was surely also liberated.

In the West, Germany was still strong, but then the Allies landed in Normandy in June 1944 and the second front was established. From that point the German army was driven back. My "masters" started quietly to remove some of the more valuable things from the house and send them away. I decided that I should run away.

It was easy enough to make the decision, but how could I carry it out, and where could I go? I did not have any friends here, although I was aware that the people of Alsace were not at all keen on Hitler's promised 'New Order' in Europe, and that they had only pretended to become Germans. In the depths of their hearts they longed for the better times before the conflict started, when everything was not so desperately short and when they did not have to send their sons to fight a war that was not theirs. But no one admitted it openly and I had no idea who I should turn to.

I decided to sound people out at a local food shop. The owners, an elderly couple, used to talk French together and once, when I was covered with bruises after a thorough beating, they had openly shown their pity and sympathy. But would they risk helping me? It could become very dangerous both for me and for them. So perhaps it would be better to do nothing and wait to see what the future held. On the one hand, I knew that the family were preparing to leave Alsace. But on the other, there was the risk that if I failed, they would send to a concentration camp not only me, but those who had tried to shelter me. Had I the right to endanger these people?

Meanwhile, Frau Frieda folded carpets, and packed the porcelain and the pictures. The house emptied. From time to time, late in the evening, a truck would appear to take away the stolen goods. Where they were going was a mystery. In the end, things happened so quickly that I had no chance to put my escape plan into effect. Once again fate decided for me. Obviously I was destined not to have my freedom. Had I succeeded, then perhaps my life would have turned out very differently.

One afternoon, this time much earlier than usual, a truck again drove up in front

Leap for Life

of the house. Herr Paul and Helmuth started to carry out boxes and cases, now quite openly without any attempt at concealment. Frau Frieda ordered me to dress the children warmly and to prepare myself for a journey. I ran to my room and tried with shaking hands to gather my pitiful belongings, still hoping that there would be a chance to escape. I intended to stake everything on one throw. But suddenly I heard Helmuth's heavy steps on the staircase. With a vindictive sneer – obviously he had read my mind – he strode into the room. "Hurry up, Mama is already waiting. You must go immediately."

There was nothing I could do. Defiance would have been senseless. Frau Frieda and the children were already sitting in the cab of the truck. I was ordered to climb under the cover in the back. One of the men who had helped carry out the boxes climbed in too. He must have been ordered to keep an eye on me. The truck started. Thus Frau Frieda began the return journey to her motherland, having neither died nor conquered, and I started a new stage in my life.

Chapter 8

Arms Factory

The journey along the crowded and bombed-out roads of Germany was dangerous and shocking. I had had no idea of how bad things were. We passed through Mannheim, Karlsruhe, and Nurnberg. These famous and once beautiful cities had become heaps of rubble. Among the ruins hovered women so grey that they looked as if they were covered with ash. They were trying to clear the rubble or to salvage belongings from under the ruins. The scene should have been balm for my soul, but somehow I felt no joy.

The journey was interrupted by air raids and took a long time, although Munich, where we were going, was not that far from Alsace. At last, at sunset of the second day, we came in sight of Munich, or rather what was left of it. I can still remember the view of the twin towers of the *Frauenkirche* sticking up like two menacing fingers above a sea of ruins. We avoided the city centre, made our way along the endless little streets in the outskirts, which were not as badly damaged, and soon drove into the big courtyard of an old mansion which was still intact.

As I found out the next day, when I helped the Frau quickly to unpack and roughly furnish the two rooms that were allocated to the family, it was indeed an abandoned manor house. Everything was on a huge scale, and particularly the kitchen, which was down a few steps. It was dominated by a large rusty stove, which had obviously not been used for a long time. In one corner was an iron bed which would now be my sleeping place. Other refugees, some from as far as Berlin, crowded the many rooms. They were mainly women with children, whose houses had been bombed.

Dreams of fortune and domination had come to an end. Boxes and cases stood in corners and were never unpacked. The Frau's eyes were often red from crying. A few days later the Herr also arrived, adding a few more suitcases to the general chaos. In one of them lay his now unused brown uniform. Obviously he was not going to obey the mad demand of Goebbels' propaganda machine to join the *Volkssturm*, the last defenders of that Reich which, not so long ago, had been going to last a thousand years.

His son had reacted differently. Still infatuated with the idea of victory, somewhere

Leap for Life

between Alsace and Munich he had joined the army, which was now made up mainly of old people and children like himself. Frau Frieda made no effort to hide her tears anymore. At last it was their turn to weep.

It began to be difficult to find enough food. The rations were getting smaller all the time. They could no longer get extras under the counter as they had been able to do in Alsace. There was no milk for the children. So the Herr got the wonderful idea of buying a goat. This friendly black and white creature was to become my roommate in the kitchen. My mistress assumed that a peasant girl like me would surely know how to milk and look after a goat. They were astonished and annoyed when it turned out that I did not have the slightest idea how to deal with the goat. So they brought in a woman who was to teach me what to do.

She prepared something in a bucket for the goat to drink, and began in a cackling voice to urge the goat to take a mouthful. The goat, which as everyone knows is a far from meek creature, tossed her head, and everything landed on the floor. At that very moment the Herr came into the kitchen to check up on the progress of my education. He slipped in the puddle and fell down very heavily. It was like a slapstick scene from a silent movie. I could not hold in my laughter and it came gushing out, as I watched him picking himself up from the floor to the accompaniment of the goat's bleating. Maybe he thought I was jeering at him, or perhaps he just needed someone to wreak vengeance on. Red-faced he yelled out, *"Du Schlampe"* (you slut), it is all your fault, you were too lazy to wipe up the floor."

I resented such unfairness, so, lowering my voice, I mumbled *"Leck mich am arsch"* (kiss my ass), not expecting that he would hear. But he did. Grabbing me by the hair, he started to punch me, taking no notice where the blows were landing. It would have ended very badly for me if the goat-woman had not been in the kitchen. She started to shout, bringing the neighbours running, and they pulled off the furious SA-hero. By then I could feel nothing since I was unconscious.

Again the word sabotage came up. He wanted to turn me over the Gestapo. But I was lucky. The phone line was down because of an air raid, and they could not call. I do not know how she did it, but the Frau got him to change his mind. She came up with the much better idea of swapping me at the local work administration for another woman – one who would know how to milk a goat!

And so my time with the Grossmans came to an end. I was still alive thanks to the anonymous Allied airman who had brought down the line. This strange switching of slaves. happening in the middle of twentieth century Europe, took place the next day. I was taken to my new workplace in the clothes I was wearing. They begrudged me even the old clothes which had been mended so many times. I was only allowed

Arms Factory

to take my boots, still with the hidden pictures. But even so I had escaped lightly. It could have been far worse.

* * *

Now the last months of the war were upon us, and I landed up in a forced labour camp. It was really a small town made up of barrack buildings, located between Dachau and Allach. In Allach there was a branch of the Munich BMW plant which produced aeroplane engines. As the bombing of Munich intensified, they moved more and more of the manufacturing shops away from the city, so the Allach branch was constantly being expanded. They had built huge production workshops in thick reinforced concrete bunkers and had hidden the most valuable machines there. Production went on at full speed, twenty four hours a day

During air raids the German workers would shelter in the bunker. For the rest of us there were only trenches, flimsily covered with boards and earth. They hardly protected us against the shrapnel, let alone against a direct hit.

People from all over Europe were herded into these barracks, which were built of thin, wooden partitions, with twenty or thirty to a room. These were called *stube* and were crammed with wooden double-decker bunks, infested with thousands of bedbugs. In each building there were toilets and washrooms, but water was always in short supply, and hot water was something you could only dream about. We worked a 12-hour day, with a 15-minute break for breakfast, and half an hour for lunch, which was served in a huge, well organized canteen. They managed to feed about 2,000 people there in four half-hour shifts. Though the food was inadequate in both quantity and quality, it was far better than the ghastly turnip soup from the shoe factory.

For breakfast, we usually had a cup of black, unsweetened, *ersatz* coffee, and a slice of black bread. It was the same for supper, but with a dab of margarine. I was hungry again, and in addition, I was beset by cold in the enormous concrete workshops. I was trained to work at a massive lathe that engraved numbers into heavy metal parts. I had to meet a quota and also deliver the parts to the next workstation. That meant I had to carry many pounds of metal a day. Constant contact with the cold metal caused my palms to get inflamed, and the skin around my fingernails cracked and opened, which was very painful.

The barracks were divided up by nationality and gender. As a Pole, I was put in the Polish women's group. Although I had now been in Germany almost two years, I was still one of the youngest workers. According to my identity card, which showed Kasia's real age, I was 18, although I was really only 16. I got on quite well with my room-mates, and if it had not been for the hunger and cold, and the constant fear of being

79

found out, I would have been much happier with my situation than I had been with my former 'owners'. At least here, after the twelve hour shift, nobody interfered with my personal life. In the barracks I was among people from my own country, speaking my own language, able to lie down on my own bed and even read tattered Polish books that had got there God knows how, and were now passed from hand to hand.

This camp was not nearly so tightly guarded as the previous one. They did not even enforce very effectively the rule that we as Poles, were meant to wear a diamond-shaped badge in violet and yellow with the letter P. Although it was quite dangerous, I sometimes disobeyed this rule. I simply did not wear the badge and so, pretending to be German, I could even take the local train into Munich on a Sunday. In spite of the war damage, it impressed me. I had never before seen such a large city. It must have been beautiful before the bombing, and even now, when most of it was in ruins, I still discovered places which were well worth seeing.

Amazingly, every two weeks we were paid a 'salary', a meagre payment and not enough to buy anything. From this small amount they deducted something for room and board and even, what overwhelming irony, for the reconstruction of Warsaw. That was the way their minds worked. They now expected us to pay for what they themselves had destroyed and which they would never in fact rebuild. We knew from the rumours which had reached even as far as our barracks, about the Warsaw uprising and the complete destruction of our capital.

As time passed I learned more of how the system worked. I discovered that within our diverse and multilingual group there was an extensive black market through which you could get anything, provided you were prepared to pay the price, which was extraordinarily high. The quality would certainly not have been acceptable to Germans, but they had their food and clothing coupons, and that market was not available to us. There was also an extensive barter trade. In return for bread or cigarettes, you could get almost anything.

I had so many needs. The first thing I bought was a pair of trousers, hand sewn by one of my fellow workers from a stolen blanket. To pay for it took an entire month's wages, and also my ration of bread, which I saved only by starving myself for several days. When the trousers were combined with my ski boots, which were battered and torn from overuse, they made me look quite grotesque, but at least I was now warmer.

Living with this new group I had to vary my story yet again. Now I told people that I came from Lwow and had been caught during one of the round-ups in a train. As in so many other instances, this small change was to have an important impact on the whole of the rest of my life.

Chapter 9

Witek. Dilemmas of Survival

One day, during dinner, two young men came toward me in the canteen. One of them, who had bushy, wavy blond hair and glasses started a conversation with me. "Excuse me, *Pani*, but I am told that you have come not long ago from Lwow ?" he asked in the melodious Lwow accent. I became confused and red in the face. Never before in my life had anyone addressed me as *Pani*, the honorary title of an adult woman worthy of respect. I started to mumble something like "Yes, indeed...but..."

But he had been born in Lwow and very quickly realised that I had only the faintest familiarity with that city. "So, you see," I said at last, "to tell the truth my home town is Kolomyja, but because I was last in Lwow and was rounded up there, everybody thinks that I am from there. I never correct them, because most people have no idea where Kolomyja is." I talked myself out of a difficult situation. For the first time in a very, very long time I had told something that was almost true. Immediately I feared I had made a big mistake. A bright warning light of fear flashed in my head. But I could not take back my words.

The other young man left and the one wearing glasses sat down next to me. I could tell that he was eager to talk. It was so long since I had talked to anyone like him. He was intelligent and widely read, so we soon started talking about books. For a second time I ignored those warning flashes, and he quickly discovered that I was no simpleton. That was how I first got to know Witek.

The next afternoon after work he was waiting for me at the entrance to the workshop. We went to supper together and then he escorted me to my barracks. From then on we did this every day. On Saturdays we worked only six hours and Sundays were free. So then we went for long walks and talked for hours.

He was seven years older than me, and very resourceful and protective. He was always managing to obtain extra food, which he shared with me. Usually I did not need to be invited twice, but tucked into everything that he offered. Almost everyone in our barrack room had a boyfriend. When they noticed that I too was spending time with someone, they accepted me more as one of them, and started to tease me, but never maliciously.

81

Leap for Life

In the meantime, I began to like Witek more and more. We were coming to understand each other better. We always had plenty to talk about, and we never got tired of talking together. Now when an air raid warning came – and the warnings came more frequently these days and the raids lasted much longer – he would come for me and we would run together to the trench for shelter. Then we would find a corner by ourselves and be almost happy, even though outside the bombs were falling.

To be honest, till now I really did not know much about sex. And what I did know seemed nasty and unpleasant. I still remembered the scene at the home of the railwayman in Stanislawow. I could still feel the weight of Helmuth lying on top of me, with his breath reeking of alcohol, his stiffening penis against me, and his tongue trying to force open my lips. So I was very nervous and frightened about the whole thing. Witek understood. For a long time we cared about each other but our friendship remained platonic. But after a time I realised that his touch was giving me a feeling of pleasure that I had never experienced before. I enjoyed it when we sat close to each other, when he held my hands, when he stroked my hair, or gently kissed my neck.

Then he started to tell me how much he loved me, that he had never spoken like that to any other girl, and that he wanted in the future to marry me. I was startled by his offer. I closed up like a snail retreating into its shell and started to avoid him. But he did not give up. Soon I realised that I was missing him. I was so lonely and lost. And for so long I had had nobody. It had been such a long time since anyone had told me that they loved me. He was so gentle and protective, intelligent and wise. I really should not push him away. So we started spending time together again.

Thus the spring of 1945 approached. The days got longer and warmer. Sometimes, although it was dangerous, we would run to the nearby forest for shelter instead of to the trench, which was where we went one April day when we heard the wail of the sirens. This was soon followed by the roar of heavy bombers. But this time they did not pass over us on the way to Munich, as they usually did. They started dropping bombs right above us. We could even see the little oblong 'eggs' dropping off the plane and falling towards us. A split second later the world around us turned upside down. Crashing, whistling of bomb fragments, geysers of earth and fire. Huge old trees were uprooted and turned into matchwood. Everything around us became a scene of roaring chaos. Witek wrapped his arms around me and we tumbled into a large crater. He covered me with his body while hell erupted around us. It only lasted a matter of minutes, although in our minds it seemed like centuries. The explosions stopped as quickly as they had started.

Then we heard the screams – our own and those of others who had been seeking shelter there. Incredibly, except for one person who had been killed by a bomb fragment in the temple, and some scratches and bruises on the rest of us, no one had been seriously hurt. I was in shock, and for a long time could not calm down.

Witek embraced me, stroked me, kissed me, and whispered gentle calming words to me... Later that day we become lovers.

* * *

The noose was tightening around the Reich. No one could doubt that final defeat was only a matter of days away. Even the Germans realised it. The Allies now had landing strips inside Germany itself, so planes came and went without warning. Everything got more and more disorganised.

Witek still kept reassuring me about his love and repeating his proposals of marriage. But I avoided answering. "Let's leave such a serious matter for after the war," I would say. "We are still not even sure that we will survive." He could not understand my unhappy mood. But I knew where it came from. My internal order of absolute silence was so strong that I could not break it even with Witek, no matter how much I trusted him. I knew that I would tell him the truth. At the right time. When I knew that its revelation would not threaten me with immediate death. But that was not the only reason I kept silent. The truth is that I had come to love him so much that now I feared losing him when he learned that I was Jewish.

Moreover, I was in constant doubt as to who I would decide to be when that longed-for freedom finally came. But I did know with absolute certainty that no one who had not been through the evil fate of our Jewish people, who had not found himself in the role of hunted animal that anyone could shoot without punishment, would ever be able to understand completely. Not even Witek. No matter how much he loved me, I knew that there would always remain between us an invisible wall, built by me because of my experiences. The memory of what had happened to us, to me and to my family, would stay in my subconscious for ever.

Now that I had spent time among Poles, even considering myself as one of them, I learned things that I had not realised before. All too often in my presence they talked about Jews and their opinion of us was always low. So I learned that we were greedy, devious, and blood-suckers in both the figurative and the literal sense of the word. That was because we ritually killed Catholic babies to add their blood to matzos. Of course there were also the frequent Jewish jokes. This all hurt me and on several occasions I tightened my fists in powerless anger. At the same time I wondered whether there was any truth at all in what they said. In their minds we were always rich. But what about the thousands of poor craftsmen who bent their backs

Leap for Life

day after day in their tiny workshops, barely keeping their heads above water? What about the families with hordes of children cooped up in one room and often with no income at all? I remembered all this very well from my own home town. The Poles never said anything about all of this.

Of course it was true that the intellect of the group I was with was not of a high level, but the fact remained that their remarks did represent the stereotypical view held by part, and perhaps not a small part, of the Polish nation. So the dilemma of whether to go back to my Jewishness, or keep forever my adopted identity, gave me a lot to think about, and I was far from sure which of the possible alternatives I would choose when the time came.

When I thought over all that had happened to us, all those pogroms and all that persecution which had been repeated over the centuries, and which could so easily happen again to a people without a homeland, I started to come to the conclusion that I would not want my children – if I was ever to have them – to be exposed to it all. I would not want them to be outcasts, wanted nowhere and accepted nowhere. I would not want them to be seen as 'the others, the strangers'. I did not want them to think in categories of 'us' and 'them' as I still did.

I loved the country in which I had been born. I loved the people who thought and spoke in my language. I knew that among them were many like Frania and Paulina. Many like that nameless peasant woman, who did not push me away at the worst moment of my life, and did not hand me over to the Germans, but rather offered her hand and helped. People like Pani Maria and her family and the many others who, with unimaginable courage, fought against the overwhelming power of a ruthless enemy.

But there were also the other kind. Those who used our misery to gain financial advantage for themselves. Those who became the Nazi's helpers in the hunt, boasting that they were better than anyone else at the task. And they were better at it, because they knew us so well. They and their ancestors had shared their land with us for centuries, so we had had time to get to know each other. Now we were hunted and betrayed, often for profit, but often just out of absolute hate. Poisoned by the Nazi ideology, they had been led by the Nazis to believe that we were totally evil and that they could arrange their country better if we were all removed.

These matters were all very much in my mind as I tried, still only sixteen, and still in my heart very much alone, to try to figure out what to do.

* * *

Indeed, anti-Semitism and the power of such people had already been growing in Poland for several years before the outbreak of the war. Among its signs were the laws limiting the number of Jews who could attend the Polish universities, and slogans like "Don't buy at Jewish Shops" and the more radical "Attack the Jews!"

At that point I was a small girl protected by my parents and by the walls of our home, but even then I was painfully aware of the atmosphere of unfriendliness. One incident in particular etched itself into my memory. To tell the truth, it was not really that important, and it does not show me in a particularly flattering light. Maybe that is why it stood out in my memory and influenced my later decisions.

Shortly before the war, in the spring 1939, there opened in our town a new play area. It was very close to the Mars cinema and offered wonderful and until now unheard-of joys. There were assorted swings, areas for various kinds of games, a basketball court and even a tennis court. There were programmes for youngsters led by skilled trainers. But at the entrance to that children's paradise, teenage Polish boys with long wooden sticks stood guard, preventing Jewish children from entering. The excluded ones would stand at the wire-netting fence with their eyes glued to these splendid activities. Their faces reflected both their longing to take part in the fun and their fear of those sticks. I felt as they did. I longed very much to be among the privileged children inside. This was the first time that I became aware how good it could be not to be a Jew. I rebelled in my heart. "I am no different from the others! Why shouldn't I be there with them? I'm not going ask anyone's permission to get in there!" Without another thought I resolutely approached the entrance. No one stopped me and I played happily till dusk.

Years later, I realised that it was not the playing that was important, but my feelings. Joining the privileged children inside, I started to feel better and more important than those outside with their noses stuck to the fence. I even thought about them with slight contempt. Why did they not dare to do what I had done? It was only later that I came to understand how easy it is to manipulate people and make them believe that, because of the shade of their skin, the shape of their nose, or the colour of their hair, they are better and wiser than others.

Although Kolomyja was grandly called the capital of Pokucie, which was a province in the Carpathian area, it was in fact just a small provincial town. However it did have very good schools, and many of the teachers were part of the elite of the town. But most of the people were very conservative and unwilling to accept innovations, particularly since they were not at all well-off. You could count on the fingers of one hand the owners of cars, or, as we called them 'autos'. Even the owners of radios or bicycles counted themselves among the most prosperous.

My brothers were not the keenest of students, so perhaps to encourage them, our parents started considering buying a bicycle. Of course there would only be one

Leap for Life

between the two of them. I remember that it was a big step, discussed for a long time in the family. Salek came up with a persuasive idea, to use the bike to deliver purchases from our shop to our regular customers. He argued that they could even order over the telephone, which had recently been installed in the shop. That black shiny box seemed to me very fascinating and mysterious. To place a call you had to turn a handle. Then the operator would connect you to the number that you asked for. I would never have dared to use that wonderful modern device, but the boys were very fond of it and, if they had not been forbidden by our parents, they would have been hanging on the receiver all the time.

Mama in particular liked Salek's idea very much. So finally the decision was made. Dad and the boys went to the shop to complete the memorable transaction. I remember with what pride they returned, pushing the sparkling chromium-plated machine, for they did not know how to ride it. Later they would take it to the Targowica where on the shores of the Prut there was a big square and there they had their "riding lessons."

Scratches and bruises apart, it turned out to be much easier than Latin or Greek, so they learned very quickly. It was a man's bike, with a crossbar on which the little one – in other words me – was carried by one or other of the boys. But the fact that they had to share became such a bone of contention between them that they came to blows. In the end Dad had to settle the turns. Pawel, as the elder, of course got to use it more often. Salek, naturally, hated this terrible unfairness and, since I was always his confidante, we discussed this "blatant injustice". My brother was even then deeply sensitive to matters of justice and injustice.

The third picture hidden in my boot, brother Pawel riding 'the bike'

* * *

The calm, somewhat sleepy, town changed greatly during the second week of the fateful German-Polish campaign of September 1939. Our balcony on the main street served as a kind of grandstand from which we could observe the impact of the war. I would stand there with Dad keeping a close watch on a sight never before seen in our town, a flow of the most luxurious cars, bumper to bumper, on their way to the nearby border bridges over the river Dniestr (Zaleszczyki) and Czeremosz (Wyznica). This was the the flight of the Polish government and its officials into Romania. Overloaded and covered with dust, the cars sped in the direction of the frontier, while horrible rumours of final defeat circulated throughout the town. This parade of vehicles lasted two or three days before it began to thin out. Eventually the cloud of dust settled. Only occasionally could we hear the roar of an engine or the honking of a horn until at last the town was again wrapped in silence. But now it was a different, ominous silence. A silence that foretold the grinding of enemy tanks and the jackboots of the conquerors. Who would they be? There were rumours about approaching Germans, and about Russians. It was then that I heard for the first time words like 'Communist' and 'Soviets', always spoken with awe.

There, on that very balcony I got from my father my first object lesson in history, or rather in political economy. It was a lesson so Jewish in its flavour that it could have been included in the famous 'collection of wisdom' of that people. Yet it was at the same time a lesson so simple that even a child like me could understand it. I keep it in my mind to this very day.

"Dad," I asked, "what does this 'Communism' mean?"

"You know," Dad answered, "till now we have had Capitalism, which means that some people are rich, some people are poor, and indeed some people have nothing. Now, if the Communists come here, they will create Communism. That means that they will take the wealth from the rich. But they will not share it with the poor, like the robbers of legend. No. Everything will be sucked up by the insatiable State of Workers and Peasants. There will be universal equality, but that will be because everyone will be poor."

It was indeed the Russians who entered the town two days later. A section of the population with Communist sympathies turned out to welcome them and their arrival was celebrated beneath our windows. But we were not standing on the balcony any more. We were hiding behind our curtains with the windows closed. The crowd with red flags welcomed the newcomers with bread and salt, according to the old tradition.

Among the crowd were Ukrainians and Poles. But most of the crowd were Jews.

* * *

In Germany it was now nearly Easter, 1945. Everything suggested that this would really be the last holiday before the war ended. The weather was already warming, and, oblivious to all the destruction around it, spring was bursting forth. The air raids eased up, but now we could hear the thunder of the artillery instead, coming ever closer.

Witek managed to get hold of some food, and we promised ourselves a picnic in the open. This time, remembering our last experience, we decided to avoid the now unforgettable little forest and went to the open fields and meadows. We spread out a blanket on which Witek proudly arranged two bottles of beer, a loaf of black bread, and some margarine. He crowned all this with a piece of yeast cake, and one hard-boiled egg, which had to symbolise the entire Easter festival. I had not seen such a treat in a very long time. It was a real feast, and the two of us consumed it on our own, dividing the festive egg between us, and exchanging our best Easter wishes.

Afterwards we lay lazily in the spring sunshine. All round us was stillness and solitude, and our eyes were soothed by the early spring green. In the nearby bushes you could hear the birds singing. One could forget that somewhere else in the world war was still raging. That the world was crazy and people wanted only to kill each other. But sadly, that was the reality, brutally brought back to us soon enough by the sound of planes flying overhead.

A few days later the German managers of the factory started to vanish. There was no one left to make us work. The machines in the workshops stood silent and idle as if the flywheel which had driven them had suddenly jammed. The last of the Germans left. The interregnum started.

Our young men organised an expedition to the military stores, which had been left, unlocked. They returned loaded with various items, mostly food. This was critical, because even our small ration of food had come to a stop. In one of the barracks we created a storage area. There we kept many kinds of food. Wooden boxes full of eggs, sugar, tea (yes, real tea), cans of meat, milk powder and even large cans of alcohol. Only bread was lacking. But we had rice, beans and flour. We elected a committee which took over the canteen kitchen and began to prepare meals there. Many of us had been literally starving until this point, and people could not restrain themselves now that there was plenty of food. They could not bear to hold back, and it was not good for their health.

In addition to food, the young men also captured some arms. They organised a militia with representatives of all the many nationalities in the camp. This meant our camp was well disciplined, unlike the situation in some others. Streets in nearby towns, empty of Germans, overflowed with a multi-lingual crowd, singing and dancing, drunk with freedom – and not always just with freedom – a crowd of people who till now had been 'forced workers'. Meanwhile, the local inhabitants were cowering behind locked doors in fear of righteous revenge.

The interregnum lasted two days. Then the first Americans arrived. Tall, well-fed, smiling, and of every skin colour from white to dark chocolate, the victorious young men approached in their jeeps. We greeted them enthusiastically at the camp entrance, waving handmade flags representing all of our nationalities, rounded up from everywhere in Europe.

Quickly the new order was established. An American Army Captain replaced the Camp Kommandant. He was assisted by the committee we had already set up, of which Witek was a member. The army took on responsibility for food and supplies. They fed us well. Sadly we were not yet fully free, since we needed a special pass to leave the camp. We understood that this was for our own safety, but it was also hard for us to accept that after everything we had been through we could not have complete freedom all at once.

The war rolled on to another battleground, but here we were now living in a completely different present. The Germans started to emerge from their shelters. It was upsetting to hear and see how they now fawned upon their conquerors. From their behaviour and what they were now saying you had to conclude that not one of them had wanted the war. That only Hitler and his clique were to blame for everything. All Germans had been forced to follow orders given by others.

Although it was not far from Allach to Munich, and I could have gone to my former masters, the Grossmans, to obtain compensation, I decided against it. I did not want to see them ever again in my life.

Because of his role as a member of the new Committee, Witek got a separate room in what had previously been the office building. He wanted me to move in with him, but I was not ready to. Although I spent all day with him there, at night I returned to the barrack room which I still shared with a few other young women. The war was still going on and I was still 'in hiding'. I was still undecided and did not know what I would do after the war ended. But I knew only too well that I was probably alone in the entire world, and that I could get support, tenderness and protection only from Witek. I knew I needed that protection very badly. In the camp, now freed from iron German discipline and the fear of cruel punishment for transgressing its commands, anything could happen. But I still couldn't decide whether or not to tell Witek who I really was.

Witek, soon after the camp was liberated, with the barracks behind him

89

Leap for Life

One beautiful day in early May we received an invitation from a friend of Witek's to come to celebrate his name day. The friend's name was Stanislaw. In Catholic Poland, unlike in many countries, there is no tradition of celebrating birthdays. Instead Poles celebrate the day of the saint after which they are named, their name day. Saint Stanislaw's day is May 8th. The guests gathered in the late afternoon. All of the people who were now running the camp had been invited, together with their female partners. The couples had all come together in ways similar to Witek and me.

I personally had no friends among the guests. Certainly I got on well with the other women in the *Stube*, but even we did not have the shared secrets or chatter typical for young women of this age. It would have been impossible. My experiences had caused me to be prematurely grown up and serious. And I was not prepared to open myself up for something so trifling as gossip. But Witek decided that after all the evil we had been through, we needed some fun, so we went along. In any case, I was curious to see what such an 'adult' party would be like.

I was particularly interested since Staszek, as he was known, and his girlfriend had rented a room in a nearby 'villa' from a German couple. This transaction served both sides. The Germans got temporary protection which provided some kind of insurance in those stormy days. Staszek and Danuta obtained comfort and privacy which would have been unimaginable in the overcrowded camp.

The owners of the house were an older, now retired couple. Their sons were off somewhere in the war. The wife assured us that all her life she had been only a "*Hausfrau*." Her husband was indeed a member of the Party, but only because he had been forced to join. Now, indeed, it was coming out that all the Germans were only a herd of enslaved sheep, who because of their inborn sense of duty and loyalty had no choice but to follow their *Führer* blindly. That they had blinkers over their eyes, and not only did not know what was going on in the conquered territories, but not even in their own neighbourhood, as at the Dachau concentration camp, for example. Where had all the arms raised in salute come from at the Hitler rallies? How had their beloved *Führer*, who had promised them a 'thousand year Reich', risen to power? But that was the way they were. Arrogant and cruel when they felt strong. Humble and polite when defeated.

The woman made available her best room, her best crockery service, and everything else for the feast. She and Danuta even baked a huge cake, using supplies we had requisitioned. The celebration turned out to be very pleasant. There was some alcohol, not too much, just the right amount to create a good mood and stimulate everyone's sense of humour. There was even dancing to music from the radio.

But to me all this seemed unreal. I was hanging in an emptiness, where everything was temporary. Even more so than when I had been living in continuous danger. And had the danger really gone? Would it ever go entirely? I still doubted it. But the desire for normal life was very strong in all of us. And the fun at the name day in some way brought normal life closer. It created the appearance of normality. But it was still only an appearance. The war, after all, was still going on.

It was shortly after midnight when the music on the radio stopped suddenly. From the loudspeaker, a solemn voice resonated. There was something special in the tone that made all of us go quickly silent and listen carefully. Our instincts were right. Because the words which came from the loudspeaker were the very ones for which we had been longing during all those terrible six years. They were the report of the German surrender, signed in Berlin that very day. They were the words announcing the end of the war!

People went crazy. They were laughing crying, shouting. They grabbed each other, embraced and kissed. And they screamed.

And the sound of shrieking reached me again. In my head little hammers started beating a familiar refrain, faster ever faster. Darkness swept over me. I was sinking into a bottomless pit and returned to the nightmare of the death train, reliving it all again.

When I came to, Witek was beside me.

"Oh God, you frightened me! Is this your special way of showing how happy you are?" Witek asked jokingly when I regained consciousness at last.

I was lying in his room, pale and tired. He had carried me there when I was unconscious, and now we were alone. Everyone else had gone off to celebrate with the other workers and with the American soldiers their shared victory, and to noisily express their happiness. Witek lay down beside me. He looked anxious.

"Can't you let me into the secret of what is worrying you so much? You always promised to tell me something important when the war was over. I know only too well that you have terrible nightmares. I have often watched you asleep, restlessly turning, muttering and moaning, and even screaming. When I ask you what evil you are dreaming about, you evade the subject and make light of it. Don't you think that now is the right time to be open with each other?"

"You are absolutely right," I agreed. "When I said I had something very important to tell you, I was talking about something on which the whole of our future lives depend. Something that will decide whether we are going to stay together or whether, even though we love each other, we have to part forever."

"Dear Kasia, don't be so deadly serious. I can't imagine, that now, now that the war is over, there could be anything that would separate us. I assure you once again that I want you to be my wife, and…"

"Wait a moment. You can finish when you have heard what I have to confess."

I took a deep breath. All my earlier doubts returned. Should I really tell him the truth? I did not want to lose him. It was so good to be together.

But no. I had to tell him the truth. You cannot build a life on lies and myths. Whatever will happen, will happen.

"I am not the person I am pretending to be. My name is not Katarzyna Raduga. I'm a Jewess." I burst out.

"But darling...." He tried to interrupt, but I would not let him.

"Let me finish. I could not bear it if at some time this were to lead to quarrels between us. I've thought about it a lot and I'm convinced the future of our relationship depends on how you react. I have to tell you. I am all alone in the world. All my loved ones have been murdered. Right now neither of us has a family. But, unlike me, you have a good chance of finding yours. I know you have a brother and a sister. Will they accept me? Perhaps they will be upset if you choose a stranger – a Jew. And that's not the most important thing. We were brought up in different situations and with different religions. It is as if everything will divide us. Right now love binds us together, but will it be that way forever? Please think very carefully before you answer."

"Don't be such a silly girl! And that's just what you're being! Whatever would make you think that our backgrounds would stop our relationship? You have no idea how wrong you are. I'm in love with you, just with you, and just as you are. Here and now. I don't care who you have been in the past, or who your parents were. I don't need to think. I know my own mind. Surely you know me well enough to know that religion is no more important to me than it is to you. Don't worry about my family. You have to live with me, not with my family, that is the only thing that matters. And I want to be with you, and not only now, when you are young and pretty. I want to be with you all my life. To have children with you. To protect you. To pour your medicine when you get ill. And to grow old together. Now I understand your moods, your nightmares, and your fainting fits. I can imagine what hell you've had to go through. If you want, you can tell me all about it. If you can't, then I promise I'll never press you. I promise we need never discuss it again. It's up to you. Whatever you want."

Witek had found just the right words to dissolve my fears. How wonderful that he had not let me down. Maybe I should trust him. I needed someone to rely on so badly. Perhaps never again need I ever feel so desperately alone. He took me in his arms. He caressed and kissed me. I gave in to the spell of his love. Our love that night found a new depth.

It was dawn when I woke. The scents of spring wafted through the open windows. The birds were starting their dawn chorus. I recalled again that earlier morning of my escape from the train, the worst morning in my life. Safe in the arms of my lover, I no longer felt horror, just an infinite sadness.

Witek moved restlessly.

"Aren't you asleep?" he asked.

"No, I am thinking"

"What about?"

"About lots of things. If we are going to stay together, we have to think about what to do next. You probably know more about it than I do, but it might be possible to go to Canada or Australia. What do you think about that idea?"

"I don't even want to consider it. I don't want to spend the rest of my life as an 'auslander'. Everywhere the foreigner is a stranger, the person at the bottom. When there is fear about politics or the economy, we would be the first to suffer, the first to lose our jobs, the victims of every oppression. After all, who are we now, and how far can we get on our own? What could we do? I still have to complete my last two years of high school. You haven't even finished elementary school. We have to go back to our country and back to school. Then we will see. I think that now, when so much damage has been done, there will be lots of work. I hope we will be able to manage. And we have to start a family."

Yes, he was right. I wanted all this so much. Learning, family, children. My own family. Yes. I liked his plan. I decided to go along with it. We would go back. To Kolomyja? No. Not to Kolomyja, although I loved that town so much. I could not live in it now, in a huge cemetery. It would be too painful to be there every day. A sudden thought struck me. Salek ! What about Salek? We had to search for him. Witek would help me do it.

"I know! We will go back to your town, to Lwow. And we will visit Kolomyja together. Its not far. But not too soon. I don't know if I could face what appears in my mind as a big graveyard of all I knew and loved."

We would visit Kolomya later. Perhaps when we already had children. Perhaps even after finding Salek.

But, on this first day after the war, we could not know that neither Lwow nor Kolomyja would be Polish anymore. Nor that the Poland to which we would return would not be the country that we had known and for which we had been longing all those years. That had been decided by others, without any reference to us.

We would soon find out how it was to be.

Chapter 10

Return to a Nation Betrayed

At the beginning of September 1945 we decided that we would indeed return to Poland, even though we knew by then that much had changed for our homeland. There was a new regime in place, and under it neither Kolomyja nor Lwow were within Poland's borders any more. They were now to be in the Ukraine, part of the USSR. Poland had been cheated yet again. Once more others had decided our fate and once more whole populations were being moved around on the political chessboard of Europe. This time it was also the Germans who, having lost the war, were now being moved from East to West.

But Poles too, who had the right to consider themselves among the victors, were also again victims. We had helped make the victory possible with huge contributions of our blood. The steamroller of war had rolled over our country several times; the tragic Warsaw Uprising had killed thousands of us and had turned our capital into a ruin. Yet now, against our will, the whole political system of our country was being changed and we were pushed under the hegemony of Communist Russia. Ours was a very dubious victory indeed.

But Witek insisted on our returning to Poland. He wanted to live in his own country, among his own countrymen. And what about me, what about Kasia, the Polish girl who had almost forgotten that her real name was Rut? Well, she was so in love that she would have gone anywhere with him.

We reached the new Polish border late in September, 1945 after another long and difficult journey in cattle trucks across war-ravaged Europe. We had no one to turn to, and we had no idea where to go for help. There were millions of people like us who lived previously in the east of Poland in what was now called the Ukrainian Democratic Socialist Republic, and had therefore lost all their roots. Like many others we were sent to a repatriation office, where we were assigned a place to live.

We were sent to a small town in Lower Silesia close to the Czech-Polish border, in the Sudeten Mountains within what were now named by the new Polish regime the 'Regained Territories.' Until 1939, they had belonged to Germany and now, under the Potsdam Agreement they were to be given to Poland to compensate for the almost one third of the country taken by the Soviets in the East. Here we would build a whole new existence. But the political bosses and strategists did not ask about the worries and anxieties of two young people. Just like it is today, that was not their concern. Like Poland itself, we had very little choice but to accept what was offered.

All our belongings fitted into two battered suitcases. One contained all our clothes, including my now legendary ski-boots. The other had some of our 'liberated' food, sugar, rice, powdered milk and some cans of meat. These were the treasures that we hauled across half of Europe and into Poland after years of slave labour. But at least from now on, here we would start our own, civilian life in a new place. We longed so much for everything to be normal. For a life without danger. For our own home with its own door, which we could close behind us and be on our own, within our own four walls. So we accepted the assignment and started on another journey, this one taking four weeks, again in the cattle trucks, which were still at this time the only transport available for people like us.

When we reached our destination, we discovered that the small town was indeed charming. It was clean, well taken care of, and untouched by war. The mountains around it reminded me of the Carpathians of my homeland. We found the two room flat that had been allotted to us. It was still almost warm from the Germans who had just left it. It was fully furnished, right down to the kitchen utensils. Thus was the circle of history apparently closed and to us at that point it seemed fair. The Germans had done much worse to us than throw us out of our homes. Now it was time for us to be on top.

But at the same time we did not feel secure and did not know for sure whether the town would remain our home. After a few years, perhaps, or even after decades, might not the tide of history wash over us again and cause another cataclysm in our lives? Endless rumours continued

With our two young daughters, Weisia (L) and Kristina

95

Leap for Life

to circulate, and for a long time life in the Regained Territories had a feeling of temporariness.

Nevertheless, we were to spend all our life together after the war in this town. Our two daughters were born there; Kristina in 1948 and, in the following year, 1949, Wiesia. I was still very young, only 20, and did not really have any idea how to handle babies. Of course I had no mother to help. But Witek's sister and our good friend Janina were always close to me, and helped and taught me a lot.

In the same small town, Witek would die of a heart attack at the age of 61. There, nearly fifty years later that phone call, which was to have such momentous consequences, would reach me.

* * *

For the first few years, I still hoped that I would find my brother Salek. So many people were returning from Russia. Maybe he would be among them. But times were still uncertain and I remained, in a sense, in hiding. More and more Poles drifted into our town, replacing the Germans who were being deported to Germany. Witek was working in the repatriation office and it was his job to find the new arrivals places to stay. He became an accepted and valued member of the small community. We got married. The ceremony took place at the local Registry Office, and I used my adopted, or to be honest, false, name. Now I could not deny that name, and anyway, I did not want to. I was still afraid.

Even though there were now hardly any Jews left in Poland, still there were anti-Semitic incidents. The Kielce[1] pogrom, for example which reignited my fears. And we would see slogans on walls and fences. I remembered vividly what I had once heard someone say, that

A stark symbol of all my anxieties, a single, toppled macewa (tombstone) in Kolomya's desecrated Jewish cemetery.

---

1 In July 1946 a pogrom took place in the city of Kielce. Forty two Jews were murdered, and another 50 were injured. It was all triggered by suspicion that local Jews had supposedly murdered a Polish boy. The Polish Government conducted an investigation into the circumstances of the pogrom. In a subsequent trial seven people were charged and the leader of the mob was condemned to death.

"everybody knows who Hitler was and what he did, but he did do one thing right, killing all the Jews." So how could I expose to danger myself, Witek, and even the as yet unborn children for which we both longed. I was constantly torn and the nightmare was not really over. At that point I believed it was the right choice to stay as Kasia.

But how could I look for Salek if I could not even give my real name and place of birth? The newspapers were full of notices from people seeking lost family members. Indeed Witek found his sister and the rest of his family, who had all been displaced from Lwow to Wroclaw, in this way. But if I put such an announcement in the paper, someone in the town might find out that I was only masquerading as a Pole, so I limited myself to writing to the Red Cross and similar organisations. But I made factual mistakes which I did not even know about at the time. For instance, my brother had always been called by his family nickname Salek. I could not remember anyone ever calling him anything else. So I assumed, wrongly, that Salek was short for Solomon. To make things worse, because I had tried so hard during the war to completely forget my own life story, I could no longer remember my brothers' dates of birth. I had changed my own so often that I was not even quite sure in which year I had been born. Nor could I remember my mother's maiden name. It was no wonder that my enquiries, based on such scanty and mistaken information, did not yield any result.

* * *

The years passed. In the 1950s the Polish government decided to register people's personal details and issue new identity cards. I realised then that this was my last opportunity to correct the record. If I did not now reveal my true identity, I would forever remain Kasia. After a lot of thought and worry, I decided I could not leave things the way they were. I could not completely deny my past. I owed it to the millions who had died. I had always felt guilty that I had survived when so many had not.

Witek accepted my decision. To change all the misinformation that I had given required a formal legal proceeding. So we went through it. Witek was my only witness. He was the only one who knew about my past. At the hearing he repeated what I had told him on that unforgettable day when the war ended. So I got a new identity card. With my real first name and my real maiden name. We also got our marriage certificate corrected. The false information was crossed out and the genuine details added. The corrections are still there in the records of the Registry Office of the town. I felt a huge sense of relief. But for Witek I always remained Kasia until

Leap for Life

his death. It was the same for those who became our close friends. They knew that I had on my papers a strange name, one rarely used in Poland. But they did not attach any importance to it. Nor did they realise that I was Jewish. Or, at least, so I assumed at the time.

In the meantime Witek, who was always interested in technical things, took the necessary courses and became an engineer in a local linen spinning mill. But his salary was very low and was barely enough to feed a family of four. We considered whether I could help by finding a job, I thought about completing my own education, but at this time it was impossible because the children needed my care and support. So we just had to accept our situation and to live on what little we had. Things stayed that way until my daughters started elementary school. My own education had been cut off violently in 1941 after only four grades. After the five year gap of the war I really felt that I knew nothing.

In those immediate post-war times many adults were in a similar situation, so special schools were set up for us. I was encouraged to get started at one of these schools, but there was nothing like this in our little town. So I had to go away by train once a week, and spend Saturdays and Sundays in a town thirty kilometres away. Week after week I went. Very often, coming back on the Sunday evening I would miss the last connection and have to walk the final ten kilometres home.

Apart from all these practical difficulties, I enjoyed this school time very much and tried hard not to miss even one day. After four long years came my reward! I graduated from the middle school with good results. With this certificate and my new skills I was able to get a job in our town – a job which had always been my dream. It was running a bookshop. Then after another few years I completed my education by getting a college degree, which allowed me to become manager of a big bookshop in the larger town nearby.

Of course the bookshop was always in a way a local political and cultural centre. 'Good books', by which I mean books other than the standard Party fare, were always in short supply, and desperately wanted by those who tried to keep their minds and hearts alive despite the deadening Communist orthodoxy. People looked to us for guidance in what to read. Once again it was books that gave me a lot of satisfaction just as I would later learn, they helped my brother to build his life and career.

But life for us was difficult. In Western Europe they enjoyed a huge economic boom, but behind the Iron Curtain we had no boom. We just had to hope for changes. In 1956 when Gomulka came in our hopes were aroused for a short time. But they faded completely after the suppression of the Hungarian uprising, which was crushed by the Soviet tanks which invaded Budapest.

Return to a Nation Betrayed

Then, in 1968 in Poland we had the Anti-Zionist campaign. Many of the few thousand Jews who had survived the Holocaust and had decided to stay in their Polish homeland were forced from their jobs and made to leave the country. Most went to Israel. At the same time there was hope of change in Czechoslovakia, but this too ended with the defeat of what was known in the world as the Prague Spring. The Soviets invaded with the help of their Warsaw Pact allies including, what we felt as bitter irony, the Polish Army.

Years would have to pass before real freedom would come.

Chapter 11

Kolomyja - A Dream Fulfilled

As for my search for my brother, I could do nothing more for decades. It even turned out to be impossible for us to go to the Ukraine to visit Kolomyja to look for traces of my family. There was also an Iron Curtain dividing us within the Soviet bloc. The Soviet government was frightened that people coming from other Communist countries would spread the news that things were better there than in the "workers paradise", and this could cause riots. So I could never even get to the logical starting place for my search.

Then, finally, in the mid 1970s the rules that governed travel into the USSR were somewhat eased. They started to allow visits, but only to family members. Witek and I both dreamed of once again visiting the places where we were born. But you were only allowed in if you had an official invitation from a relative. So we started trying to work out how to get hold of one. Eventually, after a lot of effort, not all of it strictly in accordance with the law since neither of us had any family left there, we wangled an invitation. It was 1975.

The invitation was from Lwow so that was where we went first. We stayed with the people who had invited us, a family we did not know at all, of course. To repay them for their kindness, we brought them presents of clothes and many other things that were still in very short supply in the Soviet Ukraine. Poland, although poor itself, was at that time by contrast the every essence of wealth and Western chic. On our arrival, we were required to report to the Soviet Police:

"You know that it is forbidden to travel to other towns?"

"Yes, we know," we replied.

We spent a couple of days around Lwow. Witek visited his old haunts, the neighbourhood where he and his family had lived, his school, *Wysoki Zamek* (a hill with the ruins of a castle which has a view of the whole city), the *Lyczakowski* cemetery where he found traces of his parents' graves and where many people important in Polish culture are buried. We also went to *Orleta Lwowskie*, a cemetery of great significance for all Poles, which we found had been desecrated by the Communists. It is the burial ground of the teenagers, almost children, who defended Lwow against

Kolomyja - A Dream Fulfilled

the Ukrainian Nationalist uprising just after the First World War in 1918, a group who had also dreamed of having their own country

Then we went to Kolomyja. We had signed a document which stated that we knew the consequences if we went beyond the borders of Lwow. But it didn't stop us. As we left the train at Kolomyja station, I could hardly believe that I was really back in that town. That I was again seeing the places that for so many years I had seen only in my dreams. As we walked along the familiar streets, and at last reached my old home, I was overflowing with tears, and could not move.

"Well, now that we are here, we have to go inside," Witek told me, and took me firmly by the arm. Together we passed through that oh so well known entrance. It was now over thirty years since I had last walked through it, going in the opposite direction with Pawel and my parents on the way to the Ghetto, taking with us only what we could carry. When we reached the first floor, at the doorway to what had once been our apartment, a woman appeared.

"What are you doing here?" she asked brusquely.

"My wife used to live here before the war," Witek said immediately, before I could say a word. We carefully gave the name of neighbours who had been Polish, not Jewish.

"Oh", she said, somewhat more politely, "Please come in."

That "so well known entrance"...

So we were admitted. But nothing in the house reminded me of old times. These were different people. The furniture was strange. Only the view from the windows seemed the same. And, of course, the painful memories. Unlike Witek I could not cry at the graves of those closest to me. There was only the common grave at the village of Szeparowce, where Pawel and thousands of others had been killed. Or perhaps on the cobblestones of the streets that had once literally run with Jewish blood.

* * *

It is agreed that six million died in the Holocaust, three million in concentration and extermination camps. Indeed, given that the Nazis thought big, they had created many different kinds of camps, including *Konzentrationslager, Vernichtungslager, Arbeitslager* and others. Their only real purpose was to kill. But where did the other three million die?

Szeparowce is a little village on the outskirts of Kolomyja. Like many other such Polish shtetls it was to become notorious in World War II. After two roundups, *razzias*, in the Kolomyja ghetto in October and November 1941, about four thousand Jews were murdered in the forests around Szeparowce. Also killed with the four thousand were several members of the Polish resistance. The victims had to dig large deep trenches, get undressed and "fold their clothes in an orderly German manner." Then they had to stand in a row alongside the trenches. The SS men shot everyone with their machine guns and the bodies filled the trenches. But not all were yet dead. The local farmers said later that the ground was still moving. This was how my brother Pawel was murdered.

* * *

I shuddered. We had come back to the apartment with a purpose. I had to ask if anyone knew what had happened to Frania. Or if, perhaps, during all the intervening years, someone had come asking about the family who had lived here before the war. The woman who had let us in had lived in the apartment for a long time. She had come originally from Russia and said that, when she moved in, the house was empty, but that she had learned that during the war there had been a German Officers Club here. That fitted with what Frania had said. The woman also said that when she arrived in the late 1940s there was no Fransciszka Raduga living there. And that in all the years she had been there, no one had come asking about the previous inhabitants of the house. After some thought she added that there was an old woman living upstairs, a local woman who remembered the times before the war. Perhaps she would be able to tell us something.

'Upstairs' turned out to be the flat which had once been our kitchen and nursery, where Frania had lived after we were forced into the Ghetto. But the old woman had no more information than the Russian woman downstairs. No, she did not know any Frania. No, no one had ever come asking for anybody.

I was unable to resist the temptation to ask permission to go into the old pantry. The woman nodded her agreement. I went through that door which had once been painted white, and suddenly found myself back in the land of my childhood. Here nothing had changed. The round skylight in the roof was still here. The same shelves. Even the cupboard with the large pullout drawer. The same smell. Memories of smell last longest of all.... I stayed there for a long time breathing in those scents of my long-lost childhood, until Witek became worried and came in to bring me out.

When we came back into the kitchen, the old woman looked up thoughtfully at my tearstained face and said in her broken Polish-Ukrainian.

"You know, I remember a shopkeeper family used to live in this flat. I remember them to have a little daughter...I think maybe that you are that daughter..."

That broke the last of my self control. I sobbed my heart out and hugged that old woman, gnarled with rheumatism, who had had such amazing intuition.

"Yes, you're right. That is who I am."

I was torn apart. Here was somebody who remembered, who knew that the little girl Rutka had lived here in this house and had had a happy childhood with her parents and brothers. On the other hand I realised that this seemed to dash my last hope of finding out anything about Salek or Frania, at least in Kolomyja.

When at last I calmed down, we left. The only thing we could do was to leave our address. Just in case. In case anyone might perhaps come asking. There was nothing more to be done. We kept in close touch with that family, those who had taken over our home. I felt no bitterness or anger. We had left, the home was empty, and "nature abhors a vacuum" as the old saying goes. When travel got easier, the family came to visit us in Poland, and we helped them with clothes and other gifts. Times were still very hard in the workers' paradise.

* * *

Our lives rolled on against the backdrop of worsening conditions in our country where the economic situation continued to deteriorate. Ever since the end of the war conditions had been hard, but the worst times came in the late 1970s. By that time the only way to survive in Poland was to be part of the underground economy. In the bookshop I would quietly hold back the few 'special' books for people who I knew would really appreciate them. In return, people who worked in food shops would make it possible for me to buy food and other products. Every evening I would return home on the bus loaded with bags of food. It was the only way that the whole family could eat. We Poles called the process 'organising'. The word 'buy' almost vanished from our vocabulary. Everything had to be 'organised'.

Our grandchildren were born. Still nothing seemed to change.

Through all these difficult years we were always honest in the family. We told the children about politics, and tried to analyse things within the privacy of our home. But they, like most Poles always found it difficult to keep their mouths shut. Even

Leap for Life

on the street people would make remarks about the situation. But there was one truth that I never told the children, the grandchildren, or any other friends. Up to that point no one knew I was Jewish. No one knew that I still dreamed of finding my brother.

Against this background our family was hard hit by a painful loss. Witek died of a heart attack in September 1980, just at the time when the Solidarity movement was beginning its battle against the regime. Sadly, he did not live to see the ultimate victory of that struggle and the fall of Communism, not just in Poland but throughout Eastern Europe and the Soviet Union.

Chapter 12

Rychwald. A Search Begins

Nearly fifty years after the Holocaust, I was still living in Western Poland. I was now retired, watching the changes engulfing my homeland. Both my daughters had their own families. Now I had the time to focus on my own needs. For example to take better care of my health. In February 1992, the doctors prescribed for me a visit to a medical spa. It turned out to be Krynica. Yes Krynica! I was deeply worried about confronting the place where I had spent that last carefree holiday of my life with Salek and Mama, our last holiday before the war. My fears were justified. When I got there, the memories came back with new intensity.

One day when I was wandering aimlessly along paths still familiar to me from childhood, I came upon a group of tourists who were mainly elderly women of about my age. Something about their appearance and manner caught my attention and intrigued me so much that I decided to approach them. My intuition had not failed me. They turned out to be visitors from Israel, Polish Jews who had come back to Krakow, just like I had once gone back to Kolomyja, to find whatever was left of their old lives. They happened also to be visiting Krynica.

I am not usually very quick at getting to know people or at making easy friendships. But this time it was different. At once I felt fellowship. It was amazing how well we understood each other. It was the first time in many years that I did not need to pretend. The feeling overwhelmed me. I told them who I was. They invited me to join them on their tour bus and we went together to Krakow. We went to Kazimierz, the old Jewish quarter of the city, to the Jewish cemetery and to the synagogue.

In the evening we went to a farewell party given by the Association of Polish Jews. Isolated in my little town, I had no idea that any such organisation existed in Poland. I had always thought that the purges and forced emigration of 1968 had got rid of nearly all the Jews, and that those few who stayed remained hidden and did not practice their traditions and customs.

Now I realized that I must have cut myself off deliberately from my fellow Jews. If I had really wanted to connect with other Jews, I would have been able to find them. There was no longer any excuse to keep myself aloof. Yes, it was true that I had been

Leap for Life

afraid for Witek, and for my children and, perhaps least of all, for myself but that did not justify it now. I was free, the children were grown up and had their own families. Witek had died. I had nobody depending on me. I decided to change the situation. While there was still time.

Before leaving Krakow, I got the address of the Wroclaw Jewish Association. After returning home, I went to Wroclaw and became a member. Once a month I went to the Association meeting. I also took out a subscription to the *Slowo Zydowskie*, the *Jewish Word*. But I still did not say anything to my daughters or anyone else in the family.

In the June 1992 issue I noticed an advertisement from the Lauder Foundation. It invited people to a summer camp at a place called Rychwald. The advertisement listed an address and a phone number. At that point I did not know what the Launder Foundation was. I had no idea where in Poland Rychwald was. But suddenly I felt that I wanted very much to take part in that summer camp. So I called them, and I went to the camp, and that led to enormous changes in my life.

I spent two weeks at Rychwald, two weeks that changed me profoundly. When I returned home I was able to tell my daughters about my past – their history too. Before that trip I had never in my life written anything, except personal letters. But when I came back from Rychwald I felt an irresistible need to write down my experiences. I called what I wrote, *Another Dimension*, because it seemed what was happening to me was hardly of this world.

* * *

> Rychwald. A picturesque village in the Beskid Zywiecki mountains of southern Poland. A nobleman's chateau surrounded by a large park. Modernised but still in the original style. This was where I experienced eleven days in another dimension!
>
> It was by accident that I learned about the existence of the summer retreats organized by the Lauder Foundation. As soon as I saw the advertisement in the Jewish Word I knew I wanted to be there. I called the organisation in Warsaw at the number listed in the advertisement, but unfortunately it turned out that the session was already full. But the helpful voice on the phone suggested that I should go to the source and try Rychwald itself.
>
> I know our phone system only too well, so I decided to write first. In my note I explained why I wanted so much to be there. "I have

Rychwald. A Search Begins

lived many years isolated from the Jewish community. I have had no contact with it. I had hoped that coming to Rychwald would have been an opportunity to reconnect to the Jewish community . . . and in a few days I will be calling you to see if there is any chance of a place."

To my amazement it worked. When I called they told me that they had found a place for me and that my name was now on the list. Unbelievable that anything could be arranged so easily! And that is how I found myself at the 1992 Lauder camp for the Children of the Holocaust, where I met wonderful people, where I was taken back to the world of my childhood and where for the first time after World War II, I felt free from the horror of Shoah.

After a long train journey with several changes, I arrived at Rychwald and was happily surprised by my reception. It was completely unbureaucratic. They just asked me my name, showed me my bed in a dormitory, and invited me to lunch. Feeling a little ill at ease, I began to look around. The building seemed old and historic, and I was further surprised to come upon a room which had been converted into a synagogue. I was astonished. Was I really in the right place, me, an atheist? After dinner, we got together in the community room to introduce ourselves. This was more serious than the party atmosphere you would usually find at a Polish gathering. We sat in a circle and Michael, Rabbi Michael from the United States, sat in the middle. He briefly explained the ideas and goals of the Lauder Foundation's activities in Poland and then he proposed that each of us should say a few words of self-introduction.

For many of us, including me, it was our first such experience; others had attended before. Some of us were mixed marriage partners: Jewish women with Polish husbands and vice versa. There were people of various ages and from all walks of life. We spoke several different languages and came from many different places, which might normally have divided us. But all these barriers were easy to overcome. We talked until the early hours. It was a once in a lifetime experience. That was how our integration began.

Next morning I went jogging in the park in the sun and I met Isa. We spent two hours walking, doing gymnastics and running. And all the time we were talking about our lives, past and present. In later days we were joined by Rose and our talks expanded. We moved naturally from subject to subject and there was never enough time. I met many wonderful people. Kasia; two Sophies, one from Warsaw and one from Krakow; Slawka and her daughter, Wanda, a very attractive looking grandmother; Leszek, who was a doctor and helped anyone who needed it; Dasia, a fragile porcelain figure who translated endlessly for us from English to Polish and back and was patient and considerate with all of us, and many others. At last I did not feel alone, but part of a large loving family.

And then Friday came. And my first chance in fifty-four years to celebrate a proper Jewish Sabbath. It was that long since I had, as a young girl, celebrated the Sabbath in my parents house, surrounded by my closest family, of which I alone had survived. In my parents' house the preparations for the Sabbath would begin on Thursday. On that day the noodles for the chicken soup were prepared and the challah was baked. For us children it was a special day, and even today I can remember the smell of the cakes and the potato bread mingled with that of the waxed wooden floor. This was an unforgettable mixture.

My parents were not really orthodox. At home we spoke Polish rather than Yiddish. My two brothers went to the boys' high school, the 'gymnasium', and I was in the third year in the girls' elementary school. But at home we kept a kosher kitchen and we obeyed most of the rules and traditions of our religion. My mother was always very busy with the family shop and normally did not have much time for us children. But the Sabbath was different. I remember her specially dressed up with a white lace shawl on her head lighting the candles in two tall silver candlesticks on the Sabbath table which was itself covered with a pure white tablecloth. I remember watching her hands as she performed the candle lighting ritual and how she covered her face with her hands as she mumbled the Hebrew prayer. I remember how my father would return from the synagogue and place his hands on our heads to bless us before we sat down to the Sabbath meal which always began with fish and ended with a sweet dessert. The atmosphere was that of a warm close family. In the week we were all busy, we children with school and my parents with their shop. So it was on Friday evening, and the Saturday that we all made up for the lost time spent away from each other.

So on this Friday at Rychwald, all these memories came back to me with great force when I, together with the other women, lit the Sabbath candles in the dining room. Then we greeted each other "shabat shalom" and sat down at the large table to the traditional meal. On this occasion there were a large number of guests. Everyone was welcomed and fed. Nobody worried about formalities, such as invitations or registration. After dinner we all stayed up late into the night, dancing the Hora and singing Hebrew songs, accompanied by a guitar played by a young American. A young Israeli woman, Tracy, would first sing the words, and then we would all repeat them. These two were so full of joy. I was surprised and fascinated. Why couldn't everyone else be so free and so open in their Jewishness? Free from complexes, free from the restraints which hold back we few remaining Polish Jews, free from being torn between our Jewish and our Polish identities?

We had another Sabbath the next week, but for me, this first Sabbath was the turning point. It brought to the surface so many memories; fulfilled so many dreams; this first Sabbath washed away so many nights of crying alone. But, at the same time, it broke through the barrier of silence which my experiences had forced upon me so many years before. In this circle of great closeness, I felt at last myself, at last free. I felt that suddenly I had the family that I had missed all my life. In our conversations we discovered that we all felt the same. Until this moment we had all felt branded by the lack of parents, by the lack of brothers or sisters, in one word by the lack of family. Everyone around us had somebody. We had nobody. The families we now have are created by ourselves. We had been children in an unbearable time -- now, fifty years old and more – and we decided to be family for each other.

We had many other gatherings. The rabbis talked to us about the Torah. On the last evening we had a campfire, and by its light, Rabbi Besser and Rabbi Szudrich gave us warm and wise words. They talked of the need for love between people and of the need to be good. The eleven days passed. In some ways much too short a time. In some ways a lifetime. Eleven days in another dimension, in which we could forget about everyday cares. Eleven days in another world, in the world of my childhood. After this I could take the tiny stones of memory, memories about religion, tradition, crumbs of Yiddish, and of Hebrew prayers,

Leap for Life

stones which had been stored previously in my unconscious mind through all the years, and could assemble them in a mosaic of memory. I left Rychwald as another person.

And for all this I say thank you from the bottom of my heart to all who created this " island" in which we could all meet.

Rychwald, August 1992

That was the way I experienced and described it. And after returning home I told my daughters and grandchildren that I am Jewish and I gave them what I had written to read. At first, it was confusing to them. But it didn't change anything in my relationship with them or with my Polish sons-in-law. Their reply was: "Yes, you are Jewish, and so what? Are you not the same person, our mother, who we love and know so well,"

It just took time. My youngest granddaughter Basia came with her mother to the next Lauder Foundation Camp, and was shown on Polish TV dancing the Hora. Back in our little town she was seen by all her school friends proudly wearing the camp T-shirt with its stylised Jewish Star-Magen-Dawid The star was not yellow!

So, there were immediate changes in my life. But Rychwałd turned out to lead to much more.

Because it was at Rychwald that the first real link in the chain to my brother was forged. When we introduced ourselves to each other I said that my hometown was Kolomyja, and that I believed myself to be the only Jewish survivor from that town.

Then I heard a loud, friendly and sympathetic laugh. It was Dasia, from New York, who had been translating.

"No, no, no. I personally know many people from that town who survived and now live in the United States and Israel," she told me.

Basia, proud of her grandmother's heritage

I was shocked, and at the same time, overwhelmed with excitement. "Do you really know people from Kolomyja? We have got to talk about this!" That evening we did not get the chance. But next morning I grabbed Dasia. "You said yesterday that you know people from my town."

"Of course I do. Quite a few. Besides, don't you know that in Israel there are special associations of people who come from Polish towns? Each town has a memorial book that lists the names of those who survived. I know a man quite well who is an active member of the Kolomyja Association. He is a professor at the Hebrew University in Jerusalem. If you like, I could put you in contact with him."

"If I'd like?" How can you ask such a question? That's been my constant dream."

Dasia too came originally from Poland, from a town near Katowice, I believe. She managed by some miracle to survive the war in a Nazi children's camp in Czechoslovakia, somewhere in the Sudeten Mountains. Immediately after the war ended, the few children who were still alive were taken to Israel and an aunt found her there. Having grown up and married, she and her husband moved to New York where she still lived. This was her second time at Rychwald. She was very religious and therefore she was made responsible for supervising the cooking to make sure that it was properly kosher. We became friends. When it was time to leave, I gave her a sheet of paper with all my personal information – from the years before the war right through to the present. She promised again to put me in touch with the people from Kolomyja.

We prepared to leave for our own homes confident that all the members of the group would stay very close friends. We said good bye with the solemn promise to keep in touch through our newly created association, "Polish Children of the Holocaust", so called because although most of us were now elderly, we had still been children in that terrible time.

We felt very close and since most of our nearest family and even distant relatives had vanished in the Holocaust, we, the members of this association, would now become a family for each other.

Chapter 13

"This Man Zorza..."

Dasia kept her promise Just three weeks later I got a letter. I will never forget how it started.

> *Dear Rutka!*
> *If the world had not gone crazy fifty years ago, we would maybe have become good friends. I knew your parents, and my brother was in the same class as yours in the Kolomyja Gymnasium. So I am sure you will forgive me for addressing you so personally, even in my first letter.*

It was very moving. At last I had found a person who also knew what had happened. And who could confirm what till now I knew only in my mind, that I had had siblings and parents.

The letter came from Professor Dov Noy in Jerusalem. It was the start of a warm correspondence with this man, who asked me to call him by his old Jewish nickname, Bezio. I learned a lot about him and his family. In response I wrote about myself and those close to me. He had left Kolomyja for what was then still Palestine in 1938 immediately after graduating from secondary school, when he was just eighteen. The rest of the family (and like all of us he had a huge extended family) stayed in Kolomyja. All of them, except for the brother who was at school with Pawel, were murdered.

Some time later he wrote again, asking me to search in Poland for any information about a writer whose name was Victor Zorza. As far as he knew, this was a Polish writer who was in exile, and was probably living in India. I imagined this was something to do with Bezio's work at the University. It was not so easy to get such information in the small town where I was living, so I wrote to my friend Zosia in Warsaw. She was a history professor and I had got to know her at Rychwald. I asked her as a favour to look in the National Library in Warsaw to see if there was anything there about this Zorza. Zosia tried, but she did not find much. Only that there had been such a writer, and that he had lived at one point in London. So I sent a copy of

"This Man Zorza..."

her letter to Bezio in Jerusalem and considered the matter closed.

It was Bezio who let me know about a gathering in Kolomyja of survivors, which was to be held on the edge of the Szeparowce forest on the 50th anniversary of the tragic events that had happened there. This was the very spot where mass murders had taken place. Among the thousands of victims some were Poles, but most were Jews and this was where Pawel had died.

I made up my mind. I simply had to be there.

But first I had to go to Warsaw where I had been invited to join with other Children of the Holocaust at the commemoration of the 50th anniversary of the Ghetto uprising. While I was there I discovered that a new section had opened in the Warsaw Archive Office. This was the Jewish archive where you could search for information about relatives who had lived in the territories which had been part of Poland before the war, but were now part of Ukraine. So I immediately took the opportunity to see if I could find any record of my family.

A kind clerk behind the counter listened patiently to my complex story about my ancestry, my maiden name, about gaps in my memory concerning the records of my two older brothers. He made a very careful note of everything, then disappeared. It took him more than a hour but at last he came back with a bright smile, waving some papers.

There they all were! The certificate of my parents' marriage, and the birth certificates of Pawel and Salek with all the right dates. Only mine was missing. And now I could see the correct Jewish names of my brothers, Pawel was actually named Feiwel and Salek was Israel. I stared for ages at these old and faded records which called out to me the names of my beloved nearest and dearest. So many years had passed; would they be of any help now? But that question aside, I was very happy to have them.

So after Warsaw I went on to the Ukraine. For an old woman on her own the the journey was neither safe nor easy. The Soviet Union was just breaking up. The Ukraine had just gained independence. There were difficulties getting a visa, crossing the border, and making all the other arrangements. The embassies of the countries were in chaos. But I was stubborn, and managed to overcome all the problems.

In Kolomyja I met people who had come from all over the world to the memorial gathering, indeed from as far as Australia. But I was the only person who came from Poland, right next door. It was there that I met Bezio face to face for the first time, and he said to me:

"You know, I don't want to get your hopes up in vain, but there is some reason to suppose that this man Zorza I was asking you about and your brother Salek are one

113

Leap for Life

and the same person."

I stared at him in wordless amazement.

"But he is probably not alive any more," he added quickly, before I could react in any way.

"Are you sure it's true? Where did you get such news?"

"Not long ago I attended a meeting of people from Kolomyja in Israel, and I talked about you there. One of them said that he had read an article about a writer named Zorza. In that article it gave two names for him. His original one and the one he had adopted. It said that he had been born in Eastern Poland. He has sure that this must be Salek."

"And why do you think he is not alive any more?"

"The article also said that this Zorza was on the verge of death because of his heart problems, and that the doctors were even then only giving him one year to live. And the article was written years ago."

I was very dubious. It did not make sense to me.

"What else did it say."

"That he had a family in Britain, probably a wife and daughter. That shortly after the war he had become a well known journalist and Kremlinologist, and had spent a long time in India."

Bezio standing on the left beside me at the dedication of the Kolomyja memorial at Szeparowce.

"Salek? Soon after the war. In Britain? No, that's impossible. It must have been someone a lot older than him...."

"I'll try to check it out when I get back to Israel." I was sceptical.

"All this sounds so improbable. Perhaps he is alive, perhaps not. I'm not going to get too excited about this.... No, it's just impossible. But you are right. We should check it out."

That was how we left it.

We had two days in Kolomyja, with deeply moving encounters and conversations. There was a ceremony in the Szeparowce forest, a ceremony in which the Ukrainian town officials and many town residents took part. A memorial was dedicated near where Pawel and the thousands of others died. I visited many places that were so dear to me, such as the school I went to, and our old home in which the Russian woman and her children still lived. Sadly the old woman who had lived upstairs, and who had recognised me so perfectly on my previous visit, was now no longer alive.

After those two days we separated. But it left in my mind that disturbing question. What if there was a seed of truth in that revelation? Even if 'this man Zorza' was not alive any more, his family must still be around. I knew that I owed it to myself and to my family to track it all down.

Chapter 14

Phone Calls

Back home I got a message that the next meeting of the Children of the Holocaust Association would be in March 1994, at Sorodborow, near Warsaw. Our meetings meant a lot to me, both because of the overall atmosphere and because of the particular people who attended. By now many were my friends. This time we would have guests from abroad. Among them would be Renata and Halinka from Canada and Rose from New York.

Early in the gathering, Marysia, our Vice President from Warsaw, knowing about my research, suggested that I should talk to Renata, who was interested in bringing about family reunions, and had had some successes. Renata is a very energetic and lively person, and she is always surrounded by a crowd of people. So it took me some time to work my way through to her. When I did, I immediately started on my number one topic.

"Wait a minute," Renata interrupted me. "Rose is going to London on her way home. She will be in contact with the local Jewish community. Maybe she can ask about this Zorza there. We must write down all the information, and I can explain to Rose what it is all about. She does not speak Polish, just English and German, since she was born in Berlin..." She was already scribbling things down.

"Slow down for a minute, Renata. Don't rush. If Rose speaks German, I can explain everything to her myself."

Rose listened carefully, not interrupting. She took the piece of paper on which Renata had written the details, looking carefully through them.

"But you have not listed the birth date of this Wermuth or Zorza," she pointed out sensibly.

"No, that's one thing I forgot to bring and I don't have it properly in my head. And its information you could put to good use." I was a bit worried.

"Let's do it this way," Rose said after thinking for a moment. "You are going home tomorrow, while I will be staying for a couple more days in Warsaw at the Forum Hotel." She handed me the room and phone numbers. "Please, call me immediately after you get back home and give me the missing dates." In contrast to Renata's impulsiveness, Rose was meticulous and systematic.

I was pleased, although I still did not have great hopes that anything would come of it. But I was determined not to let the smallest opportunity slip. The following evening, as soon as I got back to my flat I looked up Salek's date of birth and I called Rose. I was lucky to get her immediately. After the usual greetings, I gave her the correct dates. Then she said,

"Just to be on the safe side, please spell the name of that journalist again."

As I was spelling it out I could not think of any German name beginning with Z. So I said, "Z for Zola like the writer." I did not have any problem with the other letters – "O for Olga, R for Renata, Z once again for Zola, A for Anna. That's all." There was confusion on the other end.

"Are you sure that it is Z as in Zola. Because it is written here as starting with a B, like Barbara. B-R-Z-O-Z-A " she repeated with emphasis.

"Oh no, it is definitely Zorza. It means 'dawn' in Polish.'Brzoza' means a tree, a birch."

Renata had made a mistake. With the best intentions, but in a hurry, she made from the dawn a birch, changing Zorza into Brzoza. If it had been left that way, if Rose had not been so systematic, all the research would have led nowhere. That's why I keep emphasising the huge importance of sheer chance...

So Rose left Poland. What happened next, while I was quietly waiting in unsuspecting ignorance in Lubawka, was this.

Her stay in London proved too brief to do any research, but as soon as she got back to New York, Rose started looking. First she checked in the New York phone book. There she found Richard and Joan Zorza, with a Manhattan address. But she felt that it could not be the same Zorzas. Rose understood that Victor was dead, and she was looking for the daughter. If the Zorza daughter had married, surely she would not have imposed her name on her husband. So she made no effort to contact them.

Instead she did the logical thing. She knew Victor had been a writer, so she went to the bookstore and the library, looking in indexes and in *Books in Print*. She discovered that Richard Zorza (who of course she knew nothing about) had many years ago written a book about the Harvard student strike. She found that Victor Zorza, who she maybe knew something about, had written, together with his wife Rosemary, a book about the death of their daughter Jane in a hospice. Her last clue was that Joan, who was, at least according to the phone book, related to Richard, had written a manual on family law.

So Rose did the natural thing – for a dedicated researcher. She ordered the books from the library. When they arrived she read them carefully, and it all started to fit

Leap for Life

together. Victor, in the book he had written with his wife, described being born a Jew in Poland, and surviving in Siberia. He spoke of his son Richard and Richard's girlfriend Joan. Richard's book said on the dust jacket that Victor was his father, and Joan's book made clear that she worked for an organisation in New York. Moreover, Joan was quoted that same day in an article in the *New York Times*, further placing her in New York. So Rose got ready to call.

Richard and Joan had met many years before in the US. She was then newly divorced after a disappointing marriage, and left with two boys to bring up. Arloc, who was the younger, was hardly in the first grade at the time and Derin was only three years older. They got on well with Richard from the first. He was a few years younger than Joan and they thought of him more as an older companion than as a father. It was a relationship built on understanding. After a few years of living together, Joan and Richard decided to legalise their relationship and got married.

Joan was Jewish, but only by birth. In her home there had been little tradition or religion. Her parents considered themselves atheists. Her father was a well known mathematician, Norman Levinson. He had died about twenty years before and her mother still lived in Boston. Richard and Joan met while working for the same Quaker organisation. A few years later they started to study law.

Now in the summer of 1994 Richard and Joan had just come back from a weekend in Boston with the family. As always, the first thing they did was to go through the messages on the answering machine. One of them seemed particularly interesting. There was something mysterious in the tone of voice of the woman, who gave her name and phone number, and asked them to contact her. They called immediately.

"This is Richard Zorza, returning your call."

"Thanks. Well, let me get right into it. Are you related to Victor Zorza?"

"Yes. He is my father."

"Is he still alive."

"Yes, so far as I know." Richard was already being very careful.

"Thank goodness. Let me get right to the point then. I am just back from Poland, where I was at a gathering of a group called the "Children of the Holocaust." It brings together people who are now in their sixties, but were still children in those awful times. While I was there, I met a woman who has good reason to think that she is your father's sister. I have spoken to her, and believe that it is true. She is not sure if Victor Zorza and her brother are the same person. From what she's heard, she thinks that Victor Zorza is not alive any more. I promised to try to find out for her if I got the chance. Now I discover that he is alive. Imagine if we could bring them together."

Richard did not know what to answer. He was very confused and disturbed. His

Phone Calls

father had hardly ever talked about his family. Victor had never even told Richard face to face that he had had any brothers or sisters. All Richard knew was that everyone had died. The woman on the other end relaxed a bit.

"I have information about the family. You know, her name, the address, the names of the parents, the name of her older brother and the one that is supposed to be your father. Please write it down".

"Of course I will." The family name, Wermuth, fitted with what Richard already knew. By now Joan was on the extension phone as Rose said that this woman had managed a bookstore. As Joan said later, "If Richard's father had a sister, she would have managed a bookstore."

When Richard and Joan put down the phones they looked at each other in bewilderment and excitement.

"Well, what do you think?" Richard asked Joan.

"I don't know. We have to be very careful. This kind of news could hurt or even kill your father. I don't think we should tell him yet. Maybe we should first meet this woman and go over it all again." Richard felt that Joan was being the lawyer.

"Maybe you are right. But what if it is the truth. If so the two of them should not have to wait a minute more!"

"Yes, but you can't call Victor immediately. Its ten in the evening here, that's three o'clock in the morning in England. We can't wake them in the middle of the night with news like this. We must wait for a decent time."

The two certainly could not sleep properly that night. They dozed for a few hours and decided that the right thing to do was to call Victor immediately. They called at five in the morning East Coast time, ten in the morning in England. Richard had actually planned to check first that he had his heart pills handy. Victor answered the phone.

"Richard, why are you calling so early. It's the middle of the night for you. Is everything OK?"

"Yes, everything is OK, but something pretty stunning has happened. But do not worry, it is good news."

"Let me guess," he interrupted. "You are going to have a baby!" He had always wanted so much to have a grandchild, and he hoped that they would still do it. But Joan was already well into her fifties!

"No, Joan is not pregnant. But it is like a birth. Your sister may be alive!"

"It is possible," he replied, completely calmly!"

"Her name was Rut."

"That fits." Still completely calm.

119

Leap for Life

"Your name was Israel ?"

"That fits." Still completely calm.

"You lived at number two...." And Richard struggled to find the address.

"That's right. Pilsudski Street." Victor did not let Richard finish.

Still with complete calm they went through the discussion of all the details, and of whether to send a telegram or to telephone the number Rose had given them. As Richard said later, "It was as if he had been waiting for that call for fifty years. Maybe every survivor waits for such a call. But most wait for ever in vain."

Only after the phone call ended, did Victor collapse in tears in the arms of his partner, Eileen.

Then he tried to ring the number Richard had given him. No reply. And again, no reply.

He tried once more and at last heard the phone being picked up. A woman answered. His sister!

It was June 20th, 1994, 53 years since they had last heard each other's voices.

Chapter 15

To London and a Brother

Our questions and crying and exclamations tumbled out on top of each other. Neither could get anything clear. We were pouring out childhood memories through our tears, asking confirmation of all that we had almost forgotten. For both of us the memories suppressed for decades came rushing back and out over the phone line.

The sugar bowl on the kitchen table that we had fought over, the books we read at meals. Frania. Frania's red ribbon when my brother left home, our parents, the Sabbath. It was all too much.

Salek-Victor kept asking about our parents – of course he knew nothing. I could not bring myself to tell him. "This is not for the telephone," I kept replying, and perhaps I was right. We agreed in the end that we would call again later.

After that first call, I could hardly breathe. I yelled out of the window to my closest friend Janina, "I've found my brother." Janina knew how desperate I was to find him, and how hard I had tried.

But there was no time right then to tell her in detail. Soon Janina and my daughter Wiesia joined me; Kristina was away on holiday. They gave me medicine to calm me – I could still hardly breathe, I was so overcome.

I learned later that Victor called Richard with the news, Richard called Joan. They called their sons, and both their mothers. And of course Dasia and Rose – Bezio was in Australia, so he got to know about it later. I called my Holocaust Children friends in Warsaw. Our joy and amazement was being shared around the world.

A few short, overwhelming days later, I was sitting in a plane on the way to London. I had spent those days almost in a trance. I hardly knew what was happening to me. Salek called me every day in the morning and in the evening. Now I knew a little about him, but still not very much. I could not wait to meet him. And at the same time I was a bit afraid.

What would this well known journalist, Victor Zorza, really be like? After fifty three years of being apart, would he still be the same Salek, my beloved older brother, whom I had adored so much as a child. Maybe he would turn out to be a complete

Leap for Life

stranger, shaped by another and strange culture, and by a different language. And what would his English family be like? I had read so much about Anglo-Saxon reserve and how they did not show their feelings. How they always respected convention. Would they accept me, an ordinary Polish woman. I would not even be able to speak to them. In fact, a year ago, inspired by my first meeting with other Jews, including those who now lived in America, I had bought a teach-yourself-English book, and had started to learn the language, but my progress had been slow. English pronunciation is particularly difficult for native speakers of Slavic languages.

Such thoughts swam around in my head while the plane, after leaving Okecie, the Warsaw airport, headed for London. When the sign flashed that it was OK to unbuckle the seat belt, I made myself comfortable, and leaned back in my seat. I found the monotonous drone of the engines relaxing and closed my eyes. Like so many times before, I found myself back in the past in our old home in Kolomyja.

* * *

Salek had been the first to be taken by the war from the life of our family. After the Polish defeat of August 1939, when our part of Poland found itself under Soviet occupation, he found it a very painful experience. He had been brought up on Polish patriotic literature, and just could not understand how everything could collapse in only two weeks.

But slowly, he shook it off, and with the adaptability of a teenager, took up the new ideas, the ideas of equality and a just society, offered so falsely by the Soviet invaders. He had always had strong sympathy for the underdog and also had dreams of travel and adventure. He was of an age at which all boys dream of such things. He had always envied his non-Jewish classmates who belonged to the Boy Scouts, and he was sad that he was not allowed to belong to their organisation. So he was quick to join the newly established Communist Pioneers. Sucked in by their fine promises, he wore their red scarf and used to rush off to meetings at the Pioneer Palace. Of course, all this had been started by the Soviets, but they looked down on this boy with his 'bourgeois' background and were suspicious of his enthusiasm.

So he found himself caught between the hammer and the anvil, since at home there was a lot of unpleasantness because of what he was doing. At first Dad tried to explain to him that he should not get so involved and that no good would come of it. But when this did not work, the arguments started, to the point where Salek was fighting physically with Pawel, who did not approve either. Salek became the black sheep of the family. Things got so bad that after one final argument in which Dad

To London and a Brother

said that he did not want to know him any more, Salek ran away from home. Months passed and Salek did not come back. Eventually Dad found out that he was in a children's home in Tarnopol. He decided to go and fetch him whether he wanted to come back or not. But Salek was home for only a few days. It was already July 1941 and Hitler was about to attack his Soviet ally.

Anyway, I was not told the whole truth at the time. It was only when Mama and I were homeless and destitute after barely escaping the death train with our lives, with our futures closing in on us, that the facts came out. At the time of his first disappearance, I had been told that my brother had gone to a different city with a boarding school. When we were in the ghetto, I was told that this was possibly better for him, because he had gone with the other boys to the Soviet Union. But, that dreadful day, after escaping the death train, when Mama and I did not know what further disasters might befall us, Mama decided that she had to stop lying. She told me the truth about father and Pawel, that they had both been murdered by the Germans and that Salek had not gone to a boarding school. Rather, he had come home but left again days later, this time for Russia, ahead of the German advance, and with the knowledge and blessing of both our parents.

Mama told me at the same time, that when they were finally forced into the ghetto, they had both come to think that Salek had been right when he had tried to persuade them to escape. The only hope that was left to them was that perhaps he had managed to get to Russia, that that this would be his salvation and so perhaps at least their middle child would be able to survive as a result.

* * *

"Fasten your seatbelts, prepare for landing. The temperature in London is...."

Oh God, we are here! Was I really going to see him in just a few moments? My heart was in my throat.

With my mind still in turmoil, I followed the other passengers along the endless corridors of Heathrow Airport. Then I had to go through passport control and collect my baggage. As if to spite me, my suitcase did not appear for ages. Would it take for ever, I thought, looking around impatiently. Eventually I collected it, found the illuminated exit sign, walked through the last barrier and found myself in a huge hall full of people. I pulled off the pink scarf that we had agreed in our last phone call would be our recognition symbol and waved it high above my head.

"Its her!" I heard. Suddenly a bald man with a long grey beard emerged from the crowd and rushed towards me with his arms spread wide open. We fell into

Leap for Life

each others arms, and our tears intermingled. "Don't cry now", he calmed me with a choked voice. "We don't have to cry any longer; now we must be happy."

But how could we not cry in the face of this overwhelming joy, after all the tragedies that had befallen us, our family, and our people? We stood in a close embrace, without noticing the passage of time or the crowds flowing by. Siblings. Two children. Two children taken by the scruffs of our necks and torn apart like little puppies and thrown into the cesspool of war. Two children who, in spite of everything, had survived, and had been able to grow into adults in completely different circumstances, living in different countries, breathing different cultures, and speaking different languages.

He had succeeded in becoming a well known journalist and writer in a foreign culture and language. During the years of the Cold War he had become one of the most respected experts on Communist affairs. She had not had the same opportunities, but had used those she had. As an adult, and already the mother of two daughters, she got her high school diploma and had then trained in bookshop management. She succeeded because it was not only her job but also her passion. She loved her work. She was the right woman in the right place. Was it because of their genes that, despite having been pulled in so many different directions, they felt so close, that they still felt closer to each other than to any one else in the world? One cannot know, but that was how it felt.

They stroked each other's face and hair, as if to make sure that they were really there and to confirm each other's features. Neither of us was young any more and life had left its mark on both of us. But even after so many years that is not what we saw. He saw a little girl with a ribbon in her hair, and I saw a boy with a mop of dark hair and a lock curled over his forehead. Eventually, the spell broke. A woman with a bunch of flowers approached, my brother's partner, Eileen We were once again a couple of old people at Heathrow Airport.

"Welcome to England. Welcome to your brother's home." she said in English, holding out the flowers to me. I understood these words; they did not need translating. I understood that I was awaited and welcomed. We took the lift to the car park, and drove in the direction of their home. They lived outside London in a real English village dominated by the colours green and red, as was their house, Dairy Cottage. It was built of red brick and stood in a big old garden surrounded by an extensive area of sloping green lawn. The place felt full of tradition and tranquility. I found a peacefulness which I had not felt for a long time.

It is impossible for me to describe our first moments together properly. I just cannot remember the details. It was only on the second day, when my emotions had calmed down, when the chaotic questions and answers slowed, that I could order my feelings. That we both could.

After breakfast, which we ate on the terrace near the dining room – meals were always eaten outside so long as the weather allowed – we both settled down in the wicker chairs in the shade of the weeping willow tree, whose branches hung down into the water of a small lake.

"So now, tell me everything that happened at home from the moment that I ran away. And then I will tell you about me. Don't hurry, we have lots of time."

I knew already that he had a bad heart and that his mind functioned best early in the day, before lack of oxygen made him tired. Thinking was his life's work, and he did it intensely and exhaustingly. And in spite of his illness, nothing would keep him from this work.

And that was how we started our daily sessions which lasted a whole month, because that was how long I planned to stay in England. That was what we had agreed during our first phone talks. I had not wanted to make a longer first visit. I had been worried about what my brother and his family would really be like. I had worried whether we would be able to understand each other and whether the bonds which had held us together so strongly in our childhoods could be renewed. I was aware that it would not necessarily be the case, because sometimes siblings grow apart, even if they spend all their childhood together. And what on earth would happen in our case, when we had known nothing of each other for more than half a century?

This first morning I told him what had happened to me during the war. He listened carefully and did not interrupt once. He left his questions and reactions for the end. He knew how to ask and probe. That was how he had been able to become the person he was. He knew how to coax from someone his most intimate thoughts and feelings, sometimes things the person himself was not aware of. That was a skill he had mastered to perfection.

That evening he brought me a book. Like me, he had had two children, in his case a son and a daughter. His daughter had died at twenty five from the cruellest illness, from cancer. She had suffered greatly, but a few days before her death she found peace, both mental and physical, thanks to the fact that she found herself in a hospice. And she made her parents promise to write about it after her death, so that other sufferers would know what the hospice movement stood for and how much it could help. Because the two most important moments in a person's life are when they are born and when they die. And this was the book he had brought. Its English title was *A Way to Die*. The book had been translated into many languages, German among them , and knowing it was a language that I spoke and understood, he handed me the German version that evening.

"From this book, you can learn more about my family than I could tell you myself.

Leap for Life

and when you have finished reading it, you can ask me about it and I will try to answer all your questions." He kissed me goodnight and left the room. I opened the book. On the first page he had written a dedication in Polish.

> *'Dear little sister, it has been a long time since anyone stroked your hair; I hope we will now make up for lost time. You could not know Jane, so I give you this book filled with the thoughts and dreams of my daughter.*
>
> *Your Salek-Victor, London, June 1994.'*

I read the book right through to the end that night. When I finished, the birds in the garden of Dairy Cottage were already starting their dawn chorus.

And to think that he had written all this back in the '70s. It was quite unbelievable how similar our motives and behaviour had been. Not only in relation to our families, but also in how we evaluated our situations after the war. I had been thinking the same way, even using the same words in my conversations with my husband. I was then, just after the war, hardly more than a child, Victor was at that time older and much more experienced and, of course, also better educated. But I had Witek to support me. And Victor had been completely alone. I had always been afraid that, like so many times in the past, history would repeat itself. Now I found that my brother had been obsessed with the same fear.

Jane Zorza, who died in 1977

During one of our first phone conversations Victor asked me,

"How on earth were you able to find me?"

"Because in my mind the spark of hope that you were still alive always glowed." I replied.

There was a silence and then he said in a trembling voice:

"Rutka, are you still there? Thank you, and I love you."

I am convinced that our miracle only became possible with all the political changes in Eastern Europe after the fall of the Berlin Wall. And even then it was based on the chain of stories and good will which passed from one to another. Once again it was the help of the decent people of the world which made the miracle possible.

Chapter 16

My Brother's Story

After I had settled in at Dairy Cottage, my brother and I decided that we would spend part of our mornings alone together. Nobody interrupted our private morning talks. Not my brother's partner Eileen. Not his son Richard, who flew in together with his wife Joan from America a week later.

Richard and Joan came to England specially to meet their new old aunt. We would spend the afternoons all together. After lunch Victor rested for a while in his room and then he would join the rest of us. He had the job of translating our conversations from Polish. It was quite tiring for him, so I tried to help, using my hands, my feet and a dictionary! It was not quite perfect, but it worked and we understood each other, the way families do. We all had a good sense of humour, and knew how to laugh, even at ourselves, so the sound of laughter, although sometimes mingled with tears, was with us all the time.

The weather that summer was wonderful. Not a trace of the proverbial English fog, or steady drizzle. On the contrary, to me, used to the Polish mountains, it felt almost tropical. But in the shaded garden of Dairy Cottage it was not uncomfortable. And the house was pleasantly cool. Indeed, the cottage had originally been a nineteenth century dairy. It had been part of an estate and lay almost in the shadow of the main house, which looked like a kind of a castle, with huge redbrick chimneys. Over recent years, this main house had been converted into comfortable apartments, with modern amenities, but also with fireplaces and Victorian windows covered with characteristic latticework.

Most beautiful of all was the garden. For me it was like a dream, an oasis, a small intimate world. No noise or onlookers from outside seemed to disturb its privacy. It was separated from the world by hedges, by a glade of yew trees, and big lawns. In one corner there was a kind of wilderness, where nature was left to itself to create a primitive environment. The intertwined branches provided a paradise for birds and squirrels. The small lake was inhabited by energetic moorhens which darted into the reeds at the slightest noise. There were also wild ducks. The drakes swam together, their bright colours reflecting in the sun, while the mother ducks proudly led their offspring around the lake. They seemed quite used to people. On the bank stood an old weeping willow, whose branches formed a green canopy. Except for the terrace surrounded by flowers where we ate our meals, this place was the most beloved by all of us. Here I would sit with Victor and talk endlessly. And all our talks began with the words: "Do you remember...?" I remembered the most. During the war, Victor had suffered from amnesia. Eventually his memory had improved, but some gaps remained. Now we tried to fill those gaps together.

Early on I had asked what I should call him, by his old name or his adopted one. "You know," he answered, "all those close to me know me as Victor, so we shouldn't change it now, but in our most intimate talks, for you I will remain Salek, that boy from Kolomyja and our happy childhood years. Call me the same as our father did, as our mother did, as Pawelek did, as Frania did, all those who were pulled away so cruelly and so finally from our lives."

So that is just what we did.

* * *

My arrival had disrupted the normal routine at Dairy Cottage. I realised that my brother and Eileen could not completely abandon their busy and demanding regular lives and devote all their time to me. When Eileen discreetly reminded Victor that they had some urgent letters to write and they asked if I would mind being left alone that morning, it suited me very well. I needed time on my own to put together all that I had heard of my brother's story in the last few days. So I left the two of them busy in the study and I took myself off into the garden to sit down in a folding chair beside the pond to think it all through again.

Victor and Rosemary with their young children. This is Salek just as I remember him!

My Brother's Story

I kept wondering how had it come about that Victor and Rosemary, who had lived together through good times and bad, who had lost their daughter in her mid twenties and had even managed to write a book together about their tragedy, how had they, when they had almost reached old age, then grown apart? Now, after talking with my brother, reading the book about Jane and making my way slowly through *The Four Missions of Victor Zorza*[1] an article about Victor in English, I began to feel that perhaps he was not completely without fault in the matter, even if he would not admit it, and even though he had been badly hurt by Rosemary leaving him.

You could not say that Victor had been a protective husband. He was never willing – or perhaps never knew how – to do what was once called the "man's share of the work" in the house and garden. Rather he expected everything to revolve around him and his work. At the very time that his wife needed his presence and protection most of all as her health deteriorated, he took himself off to India for eight years. Because his work came before everything else.

Rosemary had known Peter, the man who had now become her husband, during the war, in fact before she had even met Victor. But after the war the two had parted. They just kept in occasional touch. After Peter's wife died, and with Victor away for long periods somewhere in India, they became close again. Eventually Rosemary decided to leave Victor and marry Peter.

That was the picture I had put together from the bits of information I had gained from my brother, from Richard and his wife, from Eileen. I felt that this picture must be incomplete, that there must be much more of a story. You do not so easily leave someone with whom you have spent so much of your life, with whom you have had children, and with whom you have experienced such a tragedy as the loss of your young daughter. But I also knew that I did not have any right to pass judgements. I did not blame Rosemary. I just felt that her reasons must have been much deeper than I could know.

Victor had met Eileen only a year ago. It had been a very difficult period in his life. He was hurt and bitter at Rosemary for having left him. He had practically barricaded himself off from social contacts. He even sent his son Richard away when he came one day and knocked at the door of Dairy Cottage. Victor's heart was giving trouble again, but when the doctors recommended an operation to replace a leaking valve, he refused. He would go on working for as long as he could, but apart from that his life was empty. He neglected the house and himself. Without Rosemary to care for it, the garden became a jungle. His relationship with Eileen gave him the incentive to live again. She became his full partner and helped him with everything, including

---

1 Lawrence Elliot, *The Four Missions of Victor Zorza*. Readers Digest. London 1992

his hospice work. For my brother work was simply the most important thing in life.

Victor and Eileen on the terrace, taking a break from their labours

The article he had given me described the causes he took up so passionately and outlined his life story. It had also appeared in many of the foreign language editions of the magazine. Although he did not like to be interviewed, he had agreed this time, he said, because the publicity would help what had now become his fourth mission, to establish a hospice movement in the former Soviet Union. And the article did indeed do that. But more significantly for us, this article provided one of the most important links in the long chain that brought us together. It was there for the first time that both his real surname, Wermuth, and his adopted one, Zorza, appeared side by side..

I found that Victor was reluctant to talk about his experiences in Russia. I assumed that part of the reason was the amnesia that had hit him several times. The first episode that he was aware of, had been when he was already in England and serving in the Polish Air Force. One day, he had found himself in hospital, not knowing who he was. He no longer remembered his real name, nor his adopted one, neither his actual past, nor even the story that he had made up to protect himself. His memory had been wiped clean. He explained that the doctors tried to restore it by feeding him the information in his military file, the fictional record of this 'Pole' called Victor

My Brother's Story

Zorza which didn't help at all. But as time passed, he slowly began to remember who he really was, even though some events from his more recent past remained hidden, as if in a thick fog.

He told me that the amnesia had recurred several times during the war, always triggered by intense emotions, but it usually only lasted a few hours and was never again as complete. It is possible that he had suffered the same kind of memory loss while in Russia, but given the circumstances in which he lived, no one, perhaps not even he, realised it at the time. Even now, gaps remained in his recollection of events during the period between entering Russia and leaving it. So he could never be certain whether parts of the story he told were fact or fiction and that was one of the reasons that he did not, or rather could not, tell what had happened to him.[2]

As the two of us talked, it had helped fill in memories that related to our childhood up to the point when Salek left home. That momentous event, although it turned out far better for him than our parents could have foreseen, began with a major crisis in the family. During the Russian occupation in Kolomyja, when Salek became very taken with the ideals of Communism, our parents, and also Pawel, disapproved. He was very upset and wanted to discuss it and prove to them that what he believed was right. But in those days children were not expected to argue. Children should obey and be governed by the greater experience of parents. Salek rebelled against these rules. So he closed up into himself and stopped confiding in the family, except maybe in Frania and me. But he would not involve me in such serious matters, because he knew that I was not mature enough for them.

It was only here, at Dairy Cottage, that I had learnt for the first time the full story of what had really happened. It was when I was telling him about the worst day in my life, the day when Mama had to tell me that Dad had just been killed and also confessed the truth about Pawel's death and Salek's escape. I told him how Mama had even then said that she was glad that Salek had left, because it was now her only remaining hope that he would be able to survive. My brother smiled through his tears and asked, sadly shaking his head,

---

[2] Perhaps this is the best place to correct one fact in the public record. When Victor joined the Polish Air Force, driven by the need to cover up his background, he had erroneously claimed that he had been deported to Siberia after the Russians occupied Eastern Poland in 1939. This story had been repeated and published in various places. Indeed he had largely stuck to this story right up to this time of our reunion. Now he wanted this cleared up. In fact, he had left home in Kolomyja in 1941 when Germany invaded Russia, he had somehow survived a mass shooting incident that had later haunted his dreams, and had afterwards made his way deep into Russia. He had wound up in Siberia, and from there travelled back to Central Russia where he joined the newly created Polish army under general Anders and from there via Persia to the United Kingdom.

Leap for Life

"Did she really think that? It was good of her to say it, but that's not how I felt. I have blamed myself all my life. I have felt guilty that I deserted all of you at the worst time rather then staying to save you. After Dad appeared at the Tarnopol orphanage and I returned home with him it was only a few days before the the Germans attacked. As you know, I was still infatuated by the ideals of Communism and wanted to get to Russia, which was supposedly a just society. It was then that I had the most serious talk of my life with Dad, one in which he listened to the end. For the first time I had the feeling that he was trying to understand. I told him we, the whole family, should escape from the advancing Germans, from the danger that I was convinced we Jews were in.

But Dad could not accept what I was trying to say. Why? We did not have much left after all the Soviets had seized from us, but he did not want to abandon what little we had and flee into the unknown. He was certain that all this would be temporary. When it came to an end, he wanted to be on the spot to look for everything they had taken from us. He had already experienced the Germans in World War I and was convinced that they were not all bad. He thought of Germany as a nation of high culture, a nation which had given the world great thinkers and writers such as Goethe and Schiller and so many others. Our people had managed to survive more than one oppressor, so we would survive even this one, too. But if I really wanted to escape to Russia he would let me do it. He would even put me in the care of a Russian he knew who was leaving.

At the end of our talk he told me how glad he was that we were having this conversation, and not ending in anger. 'God be with you, son' he said at last, 'and after the war maybe we will see who was right. If we survive', he added, after a while. Mama prepared some things, food, even a little money for the trip. She cried a lot when I finally left with the Russians. The man into whose care they put me was one of the Russian youth leaders. His wife was a teacher in one of the small towns not far from Lwow, so he decided to go there first, to rescue her. And that was a disaster. The wife could not be found and instead the place was swarming with heavily armed Ukrainian Nationalists, who were already settling scores with local Jews and Communists. They rounded us up and locked us in a local fire station, with many others. Then they started to call us in one by one for interrogations, which were mainly savage beatings. And that is all that I can remember. For years I was obsessed by a nightmare of people digging holes in the ground. They are all pushed into the holes. Then there is gunfire. Then there is deathly silence."

He came to a stop, but then took up the story again.

"For years I tried to reconstruct what had happened. I read everything I could find

My Brother's Story

about mass murders committed in the early weeks of the German advance, in Lwow, in Zloczow, and in the many other towns that might have been on our escape route. It was all in vain. I am still not sure what happened to me. There is still a big gap until I am there in Russia." He dropped his head and fell silent.

Now, sitting alone in Dairy Cottage garden, and thinking over everything that had happened to my brother during the war, it sank in how much he had suffered. Something terrible must have happened to him. Something so awful that his mind had suppressed it. He did not even know how he had escaped, how he had managed to get into Russia, and why he found himself in Siberia. All he knew was that he had ended up there while the war was still going on, while the Russians were in retreat, and the Germans were still victorious.

In the north, where he then was, not much had changed. Like the deported Poles and Polish Jews, he could barely scrape an existence. They lived in thin-walled wooden huts, and suffered from cold and hunger. They had to work from sunrise to sunset cutting wood. If they did not meet their quota, their already inadequate rations would be cut. During the long winter evenings, he would talk to his fellow inmates. They were not only Poles, whom the regime would consider enemies, but also native Russians, many of whom were Communists, devoted to the Revolution, but who had been sent to Siberia years ago as victims of Stalin's purges. These conversations and his observations quickly cured my brother of his utopian fantasies about Communist justice.

By this time, dreadful rumours of what the Germans were doing to the Jews in the conquered territories of Poland and Ukraine were filtering even to these remote northern areas. He blamed himself for not staying in Kolomyja to help the family. He had always had a high opinion of his own cleverness and common sense, so he started to imagine how he would return home, saving our lives, and making good his previous mistakes. He decided to run away from Siberia, to somehow get through the front, and back to Kolomyja. Of course he was still just a youngster with a head full of heroic ideas. But he soon managed to prove that they were more than idle dreams.

He did manage to escape the tundra and get to places more friendly to human existence. It was a miracle that he succeeded in what few were able to do. Maybe it is because he was still only a boy, not an adult. He wandered across the country as a homeless refugee, from Siberia to the Ukraine, where the front line was, and which the Germans had not yet fully conquered. He covered most of the distance by stowing away in dark corners of freight trains, but even managed one section in the driver's cab by making himself useful to the crew. Sometimes he hitched a ride in a peasant cart when he could get such a luxury. Food had to be scavenged and only occasionally

Leap for Life

could he sleep under a roof.

It was the peasants of Russia who helped him most. Hospitable and kind, they shared their meagre food with this homeless boy, sometimes giving him their last chunk of bread to help him on his way. It was in their cottages that he was sometimes able to spend a night, to wash himself at a well, and to rest for a few hours before he started again on this endless journey. They never betrayed him, although they must have known that he was an escapee. But he never dared to risk staying in one place for more than a few days. It was vital to constantly keep moving.

It was during this time that he became obsessed by a passion, his first passion. He wanted, he needed, to find out how such a totalitarian system could develop. He tried to understand how the Russian Revolution had devoured its own children. He started to ask troublesome questions. During his exile in Siberia he had asked his companions, the Polish and Russian Communists. Now, during his escape, he asked the same questions of the people, mostly poor peasants, who helped him so willingly. But nobody was willing to answer. The villages were quite depopulated. All the young men had been taken away to the war. The old ones did not want to respond to his questions. But they did tell him stories and reminiscences about the great hunger of the 1930s. But they always remembered to add that of course by now their lives would be far better had it not been for that accursed war which was again bringing hunger, suffering and disease.

Salek realised that he would not get direct answers to the questions that were haunting him. He would have to learn to pick up by intuition the thoughts that people dared not express in words. And he also started to look elsewhere. He looked in newspapers, in the Communist papers which were of course the only ones that were available. He looked in books, the works of Stalin, Lenin and the official histories. While there were shortages of everything else throughout the country at that time, books like that were available everywhere. So he read everything he could lay his hands on, sometimes from a library; sometimes a discarded paper lying on the floor of a railway station. Even in the most unlikely places he always had hidden somewhere in his tattered and louse-infested military coat a book or scrap of newspaper to read. The coat also served as his pillow or his blanket, depending on the need, and was really all he owned, if you excluded what could with great imagination be called shoes, for they were really just pieces of old tyres, felt and rags tied together with string .

He was beginning to read between the lines, and to understand what was not written down. He created his own picture of events and managed slowly to develop his own point of view. Perhaps he was not always right, but that was the way he learned. He had come a long way from the leftist student from a comfortable middle

My Brother's Story

class family. Life had taught him that the difference between Communist ideas of justice and their fulfillment was a yawning chasm.

After months of travelling, when he had almost reached the front line, he was rounded up with others like him and some women from local collective farms, and forced to dig trenches and set up tank traps to try to slow the German advance. It was then that he survived an air raid in which nearly all the people in his group were killed. There had been no warning. They suddenly heard the sound of diving planes and at almost the same instant, the explosions of the bombs. Salek just managed to roll down and into the ditch as the side of the road. He noticed a small concrete culvert at the bottom. Small and slim as he was, he managed to squeeze his head and part of his body in. All around people were dying. Anyone who had not been killed by the bombs, and showed any movement, was finished off by the machine guns from the diving planes. The attack did not last long, but when it was over, Salek lay there unable to move, shaken with panic and fear of violent death. It was a fear that would continue to haunt him for many years after the war. He could still hear in his mind the frightful screams as the explosions ripped people apart.

That was the moment the realisation fully struck home; he would never be able to cross the front line alive. Convinced at last, he turned round and headed back into Russia. As the Germans finally stood at the gates of Moscow, he reached the river Volga, not far from Kujbyshev. Because Moscow was in danger of capture, that city had become the headquarters of government of the Soviet Union. Salek decided that such a city would provide a good hiding-place for a refugee such as himself. He wandered through its streets crowded with refugees like him, eating whatever he could find, sleeping on the streets or, if he was lucky, on the concrete floor of the railway station. At all times he had to be careful not to be caught. At best he would be sent back into exile in Siberia, at worst into the terrible camps of the Gulag.

One morning, Salek started his day as usual reading the still damp pages of the day's *Prawda,* which were posted behind a special window outside the station, and he noticed an article by the very well known writer, Ilja Ehrenburg which made it clear he was living in the city. Before the war, back home in Kolomyja, Salek had read Ehrenburg's novels. He admired one in particular, which was somewhat anarchistic in sympathies, and which appealed to him because he too was at a rebellious stage in his own development. The book was in some ways autobiographical.

He realised that this could be his one chance to meet his idol. It would not be easy. But Salek, once he got an idea into his mind, was very determined. He found out where his hero lived, and hung around his house for several days, trying to gain entry. Eventually the novelist was confronted by a gaunt apparition who had managed to

135

Leap for Life

trick his way into the flat, burning eyes looking out from under the peak of a military cap, and a boyish figure almost lost in a much too large and very worn army coat. "I am an admirer of your books," formally announced the sixteen year-old who had materialized at the threshold of the writer's study.

"Really, and what have you read?' asked the writer, more amused than disconcerted.

The Strange Adventures of Julio Jurenito, came the immediate reply.

Now the writer's demeanour changed. That book[3], which he had written shortly after the Revolution, long before Stalin had eliminated all the Anarchists, had long since disappeared from libraries and even personal collections, because merely to posses it was too dangerous. Even he himself no longer had a copy. But Salek, unconsciously, had said the one thing that would make the writer believe and appreciate him.

Ehrenburg helped the boy. He fed him, clothed him, found him a place to sleep, and even got him a job as an apprentice at the railway works, which meant that he gained some measure of safety and some genuine documents. They became friends, and finally Salek confessed to him his greatest ambition: to become a writer, and not just any writer, but a famous one, no less so than his new friend. Ehrenburg did not make fun of the youngster's dream. He took it seriously and told him, "The Soviet Union is not the place for you. You are a Pole, and Polish Jew. You were born there, you went to school there, that is the culture you have absorbed. The best thing would be for you to go back to your homeland." He started to think seriously about how the boy could escape.

It was about the time that the Soviet government had started to negotiate with the Polish General Sikorski over the release of Polish citizens who had been deported to Russia in 1939, so that they would now join a new Polish army which would fight against the common enemy, Germany. Ehrenburg also knew of a plan to create a small Polish airforce unit which would go to England to be trained by the RAF to help replace the many airmen who lost their lives during the Battle of Britain. He concluded that Salek's best chance of getting out of the Soviet Union would be to join that unit. So he advised him to learn a few phrases of English, and something about flying, to convince the recruiting officer that he would be a good choice. "But first of all, you have to change your name," he said, "You are a Jew and they would never admit a Jew to such an elite unit. Probably many of them are anti-Semitic."

Salek accepted the advice. He went to a library, learned a few common English expressions by heart, and read as much as he could about planes, and of course

---

3. A novel written by Ehrenburg in 1921 when he was in Belgium. It had been banned in the Soviet Union since 1930.

My Brother's Story

remembered it all. He thought carefully about what his new name should be. Not many people get the opportunity to choose their own name on the verge of adulthood; most of us make do with what we are given at birth. But Salek was always an idealist. He dreamt of being a hero and of saving mankind. So he chose for his first name, 'Victor', as in victory. For his last name he decided on 'Zorza', which in Polish means the dawn. As in the dawn of hope.

That spring, when the future trainee airmen landed in England, one of the members of the unit was Victor Zorza. He was a Polish youngster who had supposedly trained in how to fly gliders while a Boy Scout and knew some English. Actually, his skill did not go far beyond saying "How do you do?" and "The aircraft is controlled by the elevator, the ailerons, and the rudder." But he did know how to announce that fact with great confidence!

After quarantine and basic training, he was sent to a Polish secondary school in Glasgow where he finally learned English, and completed his studies. In a short time his English was so good that he became an interpreter. Eventually, he was assigned to the intelligence unit of Polish Squadron 301, which was based in Southern Italy. From here the 301 flew behind enemy lines to keep contact with the Resistance in Europe, including in Poland.

The young airman devoted all his spare time to reading. He read books of history, economics, and philosophy, but above all the Communist classics. All his reading was done in English which helped him to improve his language skills. He was still looking for answers to the questions he had struggled with earlier. How could a Stalin or Hitler be inflicted on the world? What made such ruthless genocidal dictators possible? And why did they then turn on each other in the end? It was his struggle to find answers to questions like these that laid the foundations of his expertise as Victor Zorza, the analyst and journalist. A man determined to fight Fascism and Stalinism.

When the war ended and he was demobilised, my brother decided, like thousands of other Poles, to stay in England as he had no family to return to. One day Victor saw in the newspaper an advertisement for a job with the BBC. Applicants had to know a Slavic language and also have some understanding of the problems of the then Soviet Union. He knew that he had all the qualifications. Indeed, by the time of the interview he knew as much about the the subjects of the questions as the interviewers themselves. So he got the job at Caversham as a monitor of broadcasts from behind the Iron Curtain. It was here that he met and married Rosemary, a fellow BBC employee.

It was during the BBC period that he began to see it as his mission to warn the world of what he had been an eyewitness to, of what Stalin had done to his own country, and what he would do to others if he were not stopped. He read even more. He carefully studied everything he read in the Communist Party paper *Izwiestia* as well as in *Prawda*. He scrutinised not just the front page news, but everything, even the smallest and least important-seeming details. He tried to work out the relative significance of everything he read. Comparing and analysing, he would reconstruct the messages between the lines, and draw his own conclusions, trying by this method to decipher the real plans of the Kremlin. He started writing secretly for the *Guardian* newspaper (at that time the *Manchester Guardian*). This was against the terms of his contract and the BBC fired him as a result.

His writing attracted the attention of Radio Liberty in Munich which broadcast to Eastern Europe and he worked there as Director of Research for a couple of years. When he returned to England he started to write full time for the Guardian, soon achieving a column of his own called the Communist World, which brought him high level recognition and influence.

During the Hungarian Revolution of 1956, just when we in Poland also gained some hope for changes in the system, he went to Budapest and was an eyewitness to the uprising. When the Russians moved in, he had to seek shelter at the British Embassy. He had great difficulty getting out of Hungary, because he did not yet have a British passport, and of course his birthplace of Kolomyja was now in the Soviet Union.

In 1959, when Soviet-Chinese friendship still seemed in full bloom, he discovered and reported the beginnings of the split between the allies. A year later it became a public falling out. During the Czech crisis of 1968 he became convinced that the Russian army would invade. He laid out his views in his *Guardian* column, although all other experts held otherwise. After the Soviet tanks rolled into Prague, he was voted 'Journalist of the Year', the highest accolade that British journalists can award to a fellow member of their profession. The citation read 'To Victor Zorza, for forecasting with astonishing accuracy and against the flow of informed opinion the

The professional journalist, an analyst of the Communist world with a growing reputation

My Brother's Story

invasion of Czechoslovakia by the Soviet Union.'

He was indeed a forecaster of political change. In 1969, when interviewed by his own newspaper, he said, "Within fifteen years, the Communist world will adopt many of the political practices that we regard as democratic and the press will become more free." He was foretelling *glasnost* and *perestroika*.

Victor and Rosemary moved to Washington DC in 1971, where he wrote for the Washington Post and lectured about his methods of journalistic analysis at Johns Hopkins University. But they always spent their summers at home in England. It was during one of these holidays that their daughter noticed a lump on her foot. That was how her illness began. Months of surgery and chemotherapy followed the diagnosis of melanoma, as hopes were raised and then dashed. Jane died a year and a half later in the Oxford hospice Sir Michael Sobell House. With pain brought under control, she was able to enjoy her final days with friends and family. Victor and Rosemary then kept their promise to Jane to publicise the work of hospices by writing newspaper articles and the book that Victor had given me when I first arrived at Dairy Cottage. But soon after completing it, he himself was diagnosed with severe heart trouble, underwent a triple bypass operation and was warned he might have only a year to live.

Nevertheless, early in the 1980s, my brother started work on his third mission, committing himself to opening the eyes of his readers to the daily difficulties suffered by people living in the Third World. It had been Jane who had first sensitised him to the problems when she visited India with him as a teenager, and challenged her father to do something about it. Now he wanted to go back as a kind of keeping faith. He stayed in a typical, impoverished village, in the foothills of the Himalayas. He lived as the villagers did, and wrote about their lives in a series of articles called *Village Voice*. The articles were published by the *Guardian* and *The Times*, and later were translated into other languages and published in leading European magazines. The columns earned the emotional involvement of millions of readers.

Victor wrote in one of his letters: 'except for missing Rosemary, I am as happy here as I have ever been. This would be a good place to die.' But, to his astonishment, his health improved. The fresh mountain air, the simple vegetarian diet, the regular walks in the mountains, performed miracles. At one point Victor realized that it had been days since he had taken his usually critical heart medication. In the end, he spent eight years in India, taking only short holidays to go home to Dairy Cottage.

Then in 1989, on one of his regular visits back to England he stopped over in Moscow. There he met a group of Russian journalists, who had read the article which he and Rosemary had written about Jane's final days in the hospice and which had appeared in the press in many diffferent countries over the years.

The journalists wanted to show him how people were suffering as they died of cancer in Soviet-Russia. Victor was shocked. At the government run hospitals there was no place for incurably ill people. Almost nothing was being done to help those who were dying at home. There were few painkillers and the importation of the chemicals to manufacture them was severely restricted. The dying patients suffered terribly. Their families didn't even dare to tell neighbours that the disease was cancer because the belief was still strong that cancer was contagious. The very word 'cancer' was taboo.

Victor postponed his trip home. He stayed in Russia, visiting the overcrowded hospitals in Moscow and Leningrad, quickly becoming aware of the desperate need to make palliative care available to the thousands, if not millions beyond hope of cure. For over half a year he fought with the bureaucracy. They were not inclined to spend money on the dying. But, as usual, once he had made up his mind, this did not discourage him. As the article in *Readers Digest* put it:

> *That didn't daunt this slight man with a bald head and a great graying beard. And if you ask him why he – born a Polish Jew and long a British subject – is driven to alleviate suffering in a land where he himself suffered so much, his eyes blaze.* "Because people don't have to die in fear and pain", he declares, "and I can help them. In a sense my whole life was a preparation for this work."

So creating a network of hospices in Russia was my brother's fourth mission. His fourth and his final one and I think at this time the most important to him.

That's what the boy from Kolomyja who had had only a few years of schooling, had managed to achieve with his life At least that was how I now understood the story. But I still had so many more questions to ask, so much more to understand. I wondered if the month together we planned could even begin to replace our lost fifty years.

Several times I tried to come back to the subject of his memory, or rather his lack of it. But he always refused to talk about it. He would say, "I am not going to speak about things when I cannot be sure if they really happened. Although I often wonder about what events are buried in my subconscious. I think about how I was disloyal to my family and deserted you. About my fear of dying and the fear that the past could repeat itself. My daughter helped me overcome the first one. You, my sister, are the only person in the whole world with whom I can share and discuss memories of our childhood and our home. Perhaps that will help me overcome my other fears."

* * *

As lunchtime approached, I heard footsteps on the gravel path. Victor, having finished the morning's work, was approaching the pond.

"What are you thinking about, little sister? I was watching you through the window. Are you feeling lonely?"

"No, not at all. This is such a wonderful corner. I could sit here watching for hours."

"You know, Jane used to say the same thing. She also loved to sit down here. It is unbelievable how much you remind me of her. Perhaps not so much your appearance as your manner. When she was a small girl, I would see you in her."

Looking across the pond from under the weeping willow

"We don't look similar in the photographs. Maybe you saw what you wanted to see. You know, in the subconscious pictures superimpose themselves on each other."

"No, that's not it. It is just that at different times in their lives people look different."

"Perhaps you are right. I remember that when you were a boy you did not look at all like Dad. But the painting of you in the living room, that looks exactly the way I

Leap for Life

remember him. How old were you when you sat for that portrait?"

"Let me think. Maybe a bit above 40."

"So lets count. Dad was born in 1894. Mama was a year older than him. When he died in 1942 he was barely 48. Compared to us now, he was still quite a young man."

"And Pawel. He was only 21. I used to think so often about our arguments and fistfights. I regret it all so much. You know, shortly after the war, here in England, I met Pan Oszywa, who had taught us history in the *gymnasium*, and I was so pleased. He had known our family very well. Perhaps he knew something of what had happened to you all. And he did. He told me that he had seen the three of you with his own eyes, Mama, Dad and you, among the crowd being driven towards the station. He was convinced that you had died with all the others. It was then that I lost hope. That was when I gave up looking."

"No wonder... Six million..."

"Yes... Six million."

We sat together in silence for a long time. In the book about Jane there was a similar conversation. I had been struck by it, so I remembered it well. A conversation between Victor and his dying daughter. Jane was already in the hospice. They were talking about life and death. And about dying. But not just about dying. It seemed to me as if the description of his own fears was directed straight at me. Yet Victor could not have imagined even in his wildest dreams that one day his sister would be reading these lines.

> "..... what about your own family in Poland ?"
>
> " They're dead..."
>
> "Yes. I know about your immediate family, but what about the rest?"
>
> "Every one of them. Mother, father, brother, sister. uncles, aunts, cousins. Everybody. I tried to track them down after the war. It was no good. Friends of the family, even acquaintances, I couldn't trace a single one. School friends - all gone.
>
> He paused. Talking about the dead, about the people nearest to him, who were lost in the Holocaust, came too close to his own feelings about death.
>
> During the war, so long as Hitler remained undefeated, he was afraid there was always the chance he might be captured by the Germans and killed if he was identified as a Jew. After the war, when

My Brother's Story

the first detailed accounts of the horrors were published, when he saw the first pictures of the bodies of skin and bone heaped in the concentration camps, he thought not only of the past, but also of the future. If it happened once, it could happen again. Better safe than sorry. He had no family ties, no links to his past, no home to go back to - nothing that made it necessary for him to resume his identity. So he stayed as he was."

I was lost in my thoughts and did not notice that Victor was watching me carefully. Obviously he was wondering what I was thinking about so deeply. For a long time he did not dare to interrupt me, but in the end he could not hold back, and tried to change my mood.

"Rutka? Will you bake me a *kartoflannik*,[4] the sort that Mama made"?

"No, you big baby, I won't. First, you should not eat such heavy food, and secondly, I do not have the proper recipe. I tried to make it several times, and could never get it to come out like it was at home."

"You know what? We should call Dov Noy in Israel. Maybe his wife will know the exact recipe."

"No, I am sure she will not. She is a 'Sabra', born in Palestine. What can she know about an East European *kartoflannik*? You know, Bezio told me her story. Her parents came over years ago, to what was then Palestine, from somewhere in Czarist Russia. Raised in Israel, she has fought to defend the country. People like that are called Sabras. Sabra is the name of a fruit which in English is called prickly pear. The plant grows in the dry deserts of Israel and bears a sweet fruit. But the flesh is hidden behind a thick skin which is covered with sharp prickles. So you have to have patience to get to the fruit. That is why the personalities of the Sabras are supposed to be deeply hidden, and their thick skins are a sign of endurance and strong character. And that's just how they are. They spent their youth working hard, reclaiming land from the desert and swamp, building their country, constantly ready to fight to defend it. Both boys and girls. As you know, right up to the present, they still cannot put the gun away."

"Well, she can find someone who does know." I would like to send them a fax and ask for the recipe.

"Boy, are you stubborn! But it would not be the same. To get it right, you need real potatoes from Kolomyja, a proper bread oven, and local sour cream. You cannot

---

4 A local kind of potato bread very popular with Jews and others in Kolomyja.

Leap for Life

go back in time!"

"But I would like so much to smell it again."

"So I will make you potato pancakes. They smell the same."

"But it would not be the same." He turned his head away in disappointment.

Surely not, I was thinking. But I did not say it out loud. He seemed just like a little boy who could not get something he desperately wanted.

Chapter 17

Memories

The day that Richard and Joan were to leave was getting closer. They would be only two more days with us. We decided to make a video tape that would have to substitute for the time being for the personal visits to Poland that everyone would make. Victor planned to be the first to come.

I myself had already brought a video that we had recorded in Poland. We had made it in a big hurry before I left for London, mainly because I did not have good photos of everybody and I wanted so much to show my own family to my so far unknown brother. We just got together and each of us said a few words to the camera. In England we watched it together several times, and everyone said that they were sorry that it was so short and general. The English family decided to ask a friend to make a much more complete one for me to take back to Poland. By the time we were done it was almost a short feature film. It showed all of Dairy Cottage, the house and the garden, the residents and the guests. But it was Victor who had the most to say..

In Poland there used to be a saying that "He looks just like an Englishman from Kolomyja." It came from the fact that, in the 1880s, oil had been discovered near our town, actually at a place called Nadworna, and English experts had been called in to investigate. They were dressed in the typical English fashion, and soon everyone who wanted to be somebody began to dress in the same way. So the saying developed to refer to people who were pretending to be something that they really were not. Victor referred to it as he started the film with a speech in Polish to his nieces and their families in Poland.

"This is a real Englishman from Kolomyja speaking to you." He told them a lot about his former and present life, and then the camera followed him on a tour of the house. It lingered on the picture of the Himalayan village in which Victor had lived during his Indian period. Standing in front of it, he talked about his stay there and the articles he had written about the lives of the people in this Third World village.

Then we sat down at the terrace table and Victor introduced the members of his family. Everyone took the microphone and said a few warm words to their new-found relatives. Eileen, with tears in her eyes, told of our meeting at Heathrow airport, of

Leap for Life

which she was the only witness, because Victor had not wanted any publicity.

On the day of Joan and Richard's departure we took them to the airport and agreed on our next meeting. It was to be in Poland. We also talked about travelling together to Kolomyja, and that we would link the two together, Poland and Ukraine. But we agreed to settle the details later when Victor would be able to stand the strains of such a trip. Everything depended on his heart condition, and the doctors were recommending one more operation. It was already scheduled. They said that if it was a success, Victor would be fit to make the journey. The operation was to take place later that year. We were full of hope and plans for the future.

When we got back from the airport the house seemed very empty with just the three of us. But Bezio and his wife were due to come soon. For the next few days, until they arrived, we would return to normal and Victor could get back to his work. He had been neglecting his efforts to develop hospices in Russia, though the matter was indeed urgent. In fact, we had not had much time to talk about this latest crusade and hoped we would soon have a chance to discuss it.

It was important for Victor to take daily walks. Since he was an 'early bird' he would get up at daybreak and walk from six to eight in the morning. Afterwards he would have his breakfast, drink gallons of tea, then sit down with his computer and the telephone. Usually he was accompanied by Eileen, but as she was a slow starter in the mornings, she happily surrendered the privilege to me. We took our first walk the day after Richard and Joan had left.

In the grey of the early morning I was awaked by the familiar "pit-pat" of Victor's steps on the stairs, and by a tap on the door.

"Get up, sleepy head. There is a glass of hot milk waiting for you in the kitchen. And dress warmly, since the mornings tend to be cool."

You can tell each other anything during such a walk. We followed woodland paths, crossed meadows still damp from the dew, and climbed over fences. And we talked and talked. About everything. About our home. About our parents and Pawel. About hospices. And, of course, about Frania.

"Do you remember," he started with the phrase that had become our motto, "the street in Kolomyja we used to call A to B?"

"Of course I do. It ran from the city hall and then straight along Kosciuszko Street. There was a good coffee house at the end where teenagers used to meet their girlfriends and boyfriends."

"And do you remember when Mama bought Pawel a fashionable jacket?"

"Wait a moment. I can just about remember. Wasn't it a kind of green dressing gown with braid."

Memories

"That's right. I was so jealous of Pawel having it. Sometimes, when he went out I would secretly put it on. Frania warned me not to, but I ignored her. I fancied myself in it so much that I got the idea of wearing it to go for a walk along A to B. It was bad enough that I went out in such a ridiculous outfit, what was worse was that I ran into Pawel who was meeting his girlfriend there. He looked angry, but for the sake of his dignity did not say anything at the time. But afterwards, when he got home, we had one of our famous fights, in which we always got scratches and bruises. Frania would first try to separate us, and then have to deal with our wounds and bloody noses. After every one of these battles, I would have a great feeling of injustice. The first-born got everything– the bicycle, the jacket. It was the old tale of Esau and Jacob. If I had known then how it would all end...."

We kept silent for a while. Then I asked:

"What about that girlfriend of his? I remember that Pawel was very proud of her and would show off about being grown up. But I don't remember what she looked like."

"I do. She was a beauty. Wait, what was her name? Yes, I've got it, she was called Jula. I remember that her father was a wholesaler who owned a big house and garden outside the town, somewhere in Wincentowka. There were about five daughters, and Jula was the youngest. No, there was one brother. He must have been the youngest. But I'm not sure. I remember being taken by Pawel to their house once or twice. He would sometimes bring Jula home. But only when Mama was away. Because he would always keep his romances secret from Mama. Frania was in their confidence and she always liked Jula. I wonder what happened to her and her family. They probably perished like everyone else...."

"You know, when the Russians marched back into Kolomyja in 1944, only thirty six Jews emerged. Just thirty six came out of hiding from an original population of fifteen thousand. Thirty-six out of fifteen thousand. Those numbers seem even more terrifying than the six million. They are easier for people to grasp. Millions are just too many to visualise. It's too abstract."

Another silence.

"Coming back to Frania. She really must have been an exceptional woman. What courage she had to help you! And what foresight! Without her you would never have survived."

"Yes. She helped us a lot. Both Mama and me. What honesty in those cruel times! You know, when we were in the ghetto, it was only because of her that we did not die of starvation. Did I tell you that I could get out to work? In the early days after it was first established, older children could still get out. Actually, it was not so much

147

Leap for Life

to work as to be outside the walls as much as possible, since inside you could never be sure of your life from moment to moment, at least in the daytime. Although working outside was far from guaranteeing your safety, as you know from what happened to Pawel and his workmates. They were taken outside the ghetto for work, then driven to Szeparowce and killed. They were strong young men, in the flower of their youth. They never returned from this 'work'.

On a later pilgrimage to the Szeparowce forest, Richard and I saw how mature trees now cover the mass graves.

When I managed to get out, I would meet secretly with Frania. Nearly every day, in fear of her life, she would bring me some food, and I, just as afraid would smuggle it into the ghetto. You can tell from this how cheap human life was in those days. You could lose it for a mouldy crust of bread. So I would hide the treasures that Frania had given me in the most unlikely parts of my body and clothes, and I got away with it. Maybe because I was still a child. Although I could not count on that protecting me. The Germans would kill children at the entrances to the ghetto for far lesser crimes. I was just lucky. I had a lot of luck during the whole war.".

"Yes, and later? When you returned to Kolomyja from that little town, what was it called, Bukaczow?"

"No, Bukaczowce. Frania helped me a great deal. Both she and Paulina. Those two put themselves at great risk. By then there was no longer a ghetto in the town. There weren't any Jews either. The city had been proclaimed *Judennrein*, which meant that you could simply kill any Jew you came across and that anyone who hid Jews would know without doubt that they also risked being killed on the spot. It was one of the techniques intended to create a moat of moral and physical emptiness around anyone who had managed to survive thus far. You had to have great courage to oppose the system. That is why so few were prepared to help us. But all the greater glory to those who did. If it had not been for them, for those Poles who with their families risked so much, there would have

Memories

been even fewer survivors. I can never emphasise that enough. Because to this day there are still people who will not accept that any Pole failed to help a Jew during the war. Its my belief that those who deny it had no personal experience of life under the Nazis. They only heard about it from a distance, and could not take in the terrible truth, even when they were told. It is no wonder. Such a genocide is beyond the comprehension of normal thinking people. In our country, to save a single Jew took a whole chain of people who were willing to risk their lives. It was very dangerous. There were many people who collaborated with the Germans and were willing to denounce those who helped us."

"Exactly. People are different everywhere. Some are heroes and some are cowards. You can't generalise. We have had firsthand experience of both types, and what can result. In the end a person is a person and you never know how he will act in exceptional circumstances. Did you ever look into what happened to Paulina and Frania afterwards. Didn't you try to find out something about them?"

"I am ashamed to admit, no. Just the one time when I visited Kolomyja in 1975. But Frania was not there any more, and no one was able to tell me anything about her. I also went to the Targowica, but I was not even able to find Paulina's little house. Things had changed a lot by then, and the thatched cottages had been replaced by ordinary brick houses. Besides, I did not even know her last name."

"Neither did I. She was Paulina, and that was all. That's the way we talked about her, and we all knew who we meant."

"I keep going back in my mind to when I stayed in Paulina's home after I came back from Bukaczowce asking for help. You know, in spite of all that Frania did for us, there is still at the bottom of my heart this deep sadness that she did not want me even to go in the direction of our home. Logic tells me that she was right. But I still have this irrational sorrow. It was just by chance that I met Paulina in front of our building. What would have happened if I had not met her but gone straight to our flat? Would Frania then have hidden Mama and me? Maybe we would both have managed to survive. But who knows how it would have all worked out in the end. This 'what if?' does no good. Let's change the subject, or I am going to cry." We stopped at a stile and he looked intently at me.

"You know," he said, "its incredible, how our minds, even after so many years of developing apart from each other, still run on parallel paths. You remind me so much of Jane. You both have the same stubbornness. She had the same determination in the way she led her life as and finally managed to come to terms with her death, and how she insisted on teaching those closest to her, Rosemary, Richard and me, to accept it."

Victor wanted to change the subject.

"You wanted to know some more about hospices." He climbed into the next field. "You know, when Jane was dying there, she was almost happy, if you can use such a word about someone in her situation. She was at peace with herself, with us, with her fate, and with her friends. But it was not easy for her to get to that point. She suffered a lot, and went through a period of bitterness against the world in general, and particularly against us, her parents. That was a very hard time for us too. We felt that she was rejecting us, that she did not want our love any more.

Then, in the hospice she found relief. Not only from the physical pain but from the psychological one. She was dying fully conscious, at one with us and with the world. She had had time to resolve everything here on earth. And she had made us promise to write about it after she died. And we did, although it was a very painful thing for us to do. Six years ago, when I saw the dreadful conditions in which people were dying of cancer in what was then the Soviet Union, it struck me that here was a way to fulfil her last wish. So that people could die with dignity."

"I know little about these things, but it seems to me that we have a long way to go in Poland to deal with these matters. I suppose that the priests and the church are involved ?"

"Absolutely. In Poland people are very religious. They trust their faith. That helps a lot. In the Soviet Union, they took away from people even their faith, and did not give them anything to put in its place. Charities were unknown. There was nothing. Only the families who have to manage with minimal help. They even have to hide the illness, for people believe that cancer is infectious. People are afraid and react in the way people who are afraid always do. The way some do now with AIDS.

You must have some idea about the crowded living conditions that the Russians have to put up with. Imagine what its like to be bedridden. The hospitals are overcrowded, and there is no room for the dying. They get little medical help. When I saw this, I became determined to get a hospice started there. At least one in this enormous country. But I ran into big problems. Bureaucratic difficulties, medical obstruction, problems with customs regulations, as well as thousands of others.

The widespread corruption is a huge challenge. Some people smell a business opportunity. They think that the money will just roll in from abroad. I am very nervous about that, so I am trying to set it up so that the money mainly comes from Russia itself. We are just helping them to get started and offering specialist training. That's the way we are doing it. It isn't just me. There are many others who are joining in our efforts. Now there is a hospice in St Petersburg, the former Leningrad, one is just being built in Moscow and a whole network of palliative care is beginning to

Memories

spread more widely through the country."

"Sorry, but I don't understand what the word 'palliative' means. I ran into it in your book and wanted to ask about it."

"*Pallium* in Latin means a wide wrap-around cloak. So palliative care should wrap around the sick, just like a cloak. It can be used to help dying people in their own homes. Doctors and nurses who are specially trained to help relieve the physical symptoms, and to ease the mental distress of both the patient and the family, visit every day to deal with the medical care, and with all the other complex problems facing the household. This approach can enable the person who is beyond cure to remain with his family until the end, while helping to ease the suffering. It is also less expensive than caring for the patient in a hospice building, and this is often the way a hospice gets started. So in Russia...." Suddenly he stopped and took a quick look at his watch.

"I have gone on too long. I am sure Eileen is impatiently waiting for us with breakfast. We must get back as quickly as possible."

"It's not just Eileen. It's also your beloved omelette. You always eat the same thing every day! Don't you get sick of it?"

Victor always insisted on having a three-egg omelette for breakfast, made only with the whites of the egg to avoid the cholesterol in the yolk. Eileen had to fry it in a special pan that did not need oil,.

"Oh no, I don't get tired of it. I like it. I am not particular about my food. But since I do not eat meat, I must have enough protein in my daily diet."

Actually he was very precise about it. He had brought back from India many recipes for meals with lentils, chick peas and beans and also a whole selection of Indian spices. He was very careful about all the preparations. Or rather Eileen was, for she was the one who had to prepare these meals with the precision of a chemist. Personally, I felt that they put too much emphasis on it. I myself did not particularly like to cook. Certainly I was a fair cook, and my family would praise my meals, but I always tried to do it as quickly and simply as possible. I thought life was too short to waste time over the kitchen stove. We hurried our steps home.

We spoke English during our meals, or at least tried to, so that Eileen should not feel out of it. Victor was very firm about it, although I was not so enthusiastic. But I have to admit that both Victor and Eileen tried very hard to use only simple easy words. I appreciated this very much. It certainly improved my English vocabulary.

I was learning to communicate, but this took a great deal of effort. Shortly after I arrived in England, Victor had brought me a book of exercises – the same one, he said, from which he had learned English after landing in England so many years before.

151

We also bought some tapes. I would spend an hour or so each afternoon working. Then Victor would listen to what I had managed to remember, and would correct my pronunciation, though sadly often with too little result. I was better at learning vocabulary, but pronunciation was, and remains, my Achilles heel. But thanks to his teaching, we were able to continue our conversations even with Eileen.

"As we open hospices in Russia, I worry that they could become just another clinic for the elite. So I try to set them up in such a way that people of all social backgrounds will be able to get in providing they are in medical need. It is difficult and takes a lot of time, organisation and battles with the bureaucrats. It also takes money. Without that you can do nothing. That was why I agreed to that interview with the *Readers Digest*. Generally I value my privacy and I don't like being interviewed, but I agreed because I thought it would help get people involved in the campaign. It really worked and brought in both human and financial resources."

"Don't forget how it helped bring us together. It was there your real name was published for the first time. It did two things. On the one hand it helped your British Russian Hospice Society. On the other –"

"You're absolutely right to use the word 'your'". Eileen broke into the conversation. "The Society may have famous patrons like Margaret Thatcher, the Archbishop of Canterbury and the head of the Russian Orthodox Church, but the fact is that its only Victor who gets things done. He is the driving force behind the whole enterprise. If it were not for his constant efforts, nothing would happen. The workload gets heavier all the time. It takes more and more out of him, and his health won't stand up to the strain."

"Don't fuss. Who was it who went with me to Moscow and helped me organise everything. You know perfectly well that without you I would not be able to do much."

"Well stop trying to outdo each other," I interrupted their argument. "Let's just say that you both keep things moving. And you have managed to come pretty far with it and also, like me to create a human chain not only of important people, but also of ordinary people who want to help."

"Yes, I have to admit that your brother has the strength to handle those difficult conditions and lots of other problems. But he pays too high a price. He pays with his heart condition," Eileen repeated her concerns.

"But the two of you still do not understand. It's worth the price. Imagine being able to help even one person who is going to die in pain and fear. It is worth it for just one person. And what if you can help dozens or even hundreds? From that viewpoint, how can you argue that the health of one individual is more important?"

Memories

That was Victor. With a sentence or two he ended the debate. Because, as usual, he was right. I was to learn later that when he had been a refugee in Russia over fifty years before, he had been befriended by people in the towns of Tula and Omsk. One woman who took him in for a few days was herself in the last stages of cancer. It is no coincidence that both these towns now have a hospice. My brother had not forgotten his debt.

Those dedicated to hospices make their own chain of compassion. Our lives have many parallels indeed.

Chapter 18

Bezio, Jula, Frania and the Righteous Gentiles

The time until our guests were to arrive passed quickly and on Saturday Eileen and I drove to the airport to pick up Bezio and his wife Tamar. Victor stayed home. He did not like the noisy and crowded terminal. Besides, it would not have been convenient to have five in the little car. We did not talk much on the way. Eileen had to concentrate on the heavy traffic, so I had time to think things over.

I had wondered what Tamar would be like. I had come to know Bezio mainly through correspondence, but also during our visit to Kolomya. Bezio told me she was not much interested in the matters of 'the old country', since she is a 'Sabra'. So I was very curious about Tamar. Just as well that I now had a smattering of English, and we would be able to talk to each other. And there would be two interpreters, Victor and Bezio. We got back to Dairy Cottage in time for lunch. Our guests were to stay for the weekend. On Monday Dov was to give a lecture in London, so we had a day and a half together.

They settled into their room, refreshed themselves, and then came down to the terrace. Victor and Bezio got on immediately, as if they had known each other for hundreds of years. They had a lot in common, but in particular the slang of Kolomyja. Tamar turned out to be very warm. I could not see any of the supposed Sabra prickliness or brusqueness. Even though Victor should have been taking his afternoon nap, he was very talkative and lively that day.

Tamar was an archaeologist. She spoke English very well. After Hebrew it is Israel's second language. She had studied in England, and knew the country and its customs. She had a good sense of humour and spoke very interestingly about her work. No wonder. She lived in a country in which every handful of earth is full of history. It had been the cradle of three of the world's most powerful religions, which had spread to every corner of the earth. Almost every spadeful brought to light new revelations.

At last our conversation came round to what was most interesting of all to us, our reunion, in which Bezio had played such an important role.

"I have to tell you that the key to the whole amazing story was really an article in the Israeli paper *Ma'ariv*, and the confusion about Victor-Salek's death was caused by a mistranslation into Hebrew because some of our vowels have the same sound but different meanings. That can happen easily if the translator is not skilled. But I have one question for you." He turned to Victor.

"That adventure with Ehrenburg. It sounds so unlikely. Did it really happen that way? Or did your writer's imagination carry you away?"

"Oh no. There is no doubt about it. I did have amnesia during the war, and some strange things happened with my memory. It's like standing on a mountain top, say in the Himalayas. Some of the summits are covered in mist, others are totally clear. But the incident with Ehrenburg is one of the clearest in my mind. I have never lost the memory, it was one of the most important events in my life. I can even remember the woman who opened the door of his house when I first knocked on it. She had a moustache. She blew up at me the way Russians do and ordered me to clear out. So I waited around for another chance.

When I saw Ehrenburg return home I knocked once again. There was a loud exchange of words between me and the woman. From the depths of the house I heard a voice. "What the hell is going on?" I simply slipped round her and ran into the room the voice was coming from. It was huge, and almost empty, except for a large carpet covering almost all the floor and a big desk in one corner. Behind the desk he, Ehrenburg, sat. I knew him only from his writings, and did not know his face. I was confused and did not even dare to lift up my head. All I could see behind the desk were his feet – which were wearing *walonki*. Can you imagine what that meant for someone like me, real *walonki* boots? They were not the usual felt boots. No, they were made of tiger skin! I lifted my eyes to the face of the man who was wearing such extraordinary boots. Do you know what was my first impression of the features of that face? It was kindness. Above all kindness. That encouraged me. Well, the rest was the same as I described many years ago in the book about Jane and then repeated it for the *Readers' Digest*."

"But my question is whether you met him again after the war," I asked.

"Another good question. Yes. I did, but just once. He came over to England, years after the war. When I heard about it, I wanted very much to meet him again. Although it was not easy, I managed to get an invitation to a banquet given in his honour. I squeezed myself into a formal jacket, which I hated doing. But my hero was surrounded at all times by a crowd of bodyguards. When at last I managed to get through to him, I introduced myself and said: "It is me. The boy whom you helped once in Russia." He looked me over from head to toe and said with little interest, "Indeed, I do not remember. Besides, you know, I helped many people." That was it.

Leap for Life

But I felt that behind the mask of indifference, I could see his familiar ironic smile. Apparently the bodyguards were there to guard more than his safety."

All this time I had been wondering what the important news could be that Bezio had said he was bringing. At last I could bear it no longer and enquired innocently, "How was your trip to the States?"

"It was excellent. We went to Florida. But at this time of the year it is unbearably hot," Tamar answered kindly, looking knowingly at Bezio, as if to remind him of something.

"I have some important news, but I really do not know how to start," he said in answer to her silent message. "Because it is so extraordinary and very moving."

"So just get started, Bezio. Do you really think, after everything that has happened to us, that you will be able to surprise us," Victor said jokingly.

"I wouldn't bet on that! In Israel, when the news got around about your reunion, someone came up with another piece of information. He told me that the girl – now the elderly woman – who was once Pawel's fiancée, is living in Florida. Do you remember her? Her name is Jula."

"Of course we do. Rutka and I were talking about her just a few days ago. She survived? That is marvellous. We must contact her!"

"I have done so already, on your behalf. I met her in Florida and we had a long talk. She is married and the mother of two children. She and her husband used to live in New York, where they started a successful business. Like many Americans, they retired to Florida."

"Get to the point. How did she manage to survive ?" I lost my patience.

"That's what I have to tell you. She was saved by Frania. Your Frania."

"What!"

"That's right. Your Frania. Jula told me everything. I have a letter from her to the two of you."

He reached into the pocket of his jacket, which was hanging from the back of his chair, and got out an envelope. The envelope was not sealed. A small black and white photograph, yellowed at the edges, fell out. The picture was of a fourteen year old boy wearing a dark school uniform with a high stiff collar and two silver stripes. On the back of the photo, in faded familiar writing, was the inscription, "To dear Jula as a keepsake – from Pawel." And then his signature and the date, June 1941. Suddenly another memory came back. I remembered both my brothers practising their signatures, scrawling over endless sheets of paper until they were perfect.

From the picture Jula had kept, a childish, round, but very serious face gazed out at us. In some ways it was similar to the identity card picture that had been taken of me

Bezio, Jula, Frania and the Righteous Gentiles

that eventful day in Germany. In my picture I was only fifteen, but the eyes were full of sadness, no childishness remained. How the past calls to us in unexpected ways! What else would it bring us? I reached with shaking hands for the letter and started to read in Polish as my voice broke:

> My dears,
> Bezio has told me about your wonderful reunion. After so many years, I am happy for you. I also can never forget those days. It is thanks to your family, thanks to Pawel, that I managed to survive the Shoah. Me and my youngest brother. It was your Frania who managed to hide us. In your pantry. In the large cupboard which I am sure you remember. We stayed there 20 months – an eternity. From the autumn of 1942 until the Soviets came back to Kolomyja. I do not need to explain to you what this all meant. No one else could really understand.
>
> Now let me tell you how it all happened. You must remember how the Germans had ordered all those of us left in the ghetto to register at the court building of the Jewish Council, the Judenrat. It was just a ruse to gather everyone together in one place at the same time, and thousands were caught in that trap. It was the roundup in which you, Rutka, your parents and so many others were taken away. By then, only my younger brother and I were left out of our large family. I did not believe what the Germans said about the 'Registration', so I decided not to obey the order. We went with a few others into a hiding place inside the ghetto that had been prepared for such an event. That way we survived the roundup itself, but we could not stay there long

> because the Germans then set the ghetto on fire. We had to look for another shelter.
>
> You also surely know that Pawel was killed at Szeparowce. He was forced there with a whole group of young people who were working outside the ghetto. One day they went to their work and never came back. But before that happened, Pawel had said to me, "If you are ever trapped and need help, you can always turn to Frania." So when my brother and I came out of the bunker we decided to try to reach her. It was not easy, but we made it.
>
> By then she already knew what had happened. She knew that the three of you had been taken away in the death train. So she decided she would try at least to save us. It was then that she took us into the home that was once yours and hid us in the big cupboard in the pantry."

I stopped. Tears rolled down my cheeks. So that was the reason that Frania was so opposed to my going to Pilsudski Street when I was staying at Paulina's place. By then Jula and her brother were already hiding there! That explained so much...

Bezio gently took the letter from my hand and continued to read. Eileen looked on with some concern. We were speaking Polish, so she could not follow what was happening. Tamar knew something in advance from Bezio. But they both sensed that something sad and significant was coming to light, something to do with the past of the siblings.

> "Then Frania told me that you had arrived, that the two of you had managed to escape the train and that you were at Paulina's place. And that instead of being happy she was in despair, because she did not know what to do. It was I who suggested the idea of Germany. I knew of some girls who had pulled it off. I myself would have done it if it were not for my little brother. He was the only one left, and I had to save him.
>
> You know what happened. You left and we waited day after day for a message. It took a long time, but at last it came. We were so happy that you had succeeded and that your Mama was safe at the Treuhander. It lifted a weight from Frania's heart, for she had qualms of conscience. It hurt to see how unhappy she was. She was a very unusual woman, very bound to your family. She used to tell me how well your mother had treated her, how she had planned to help Frania bring her daughter

to Kolomyja and perhaps work on her own account one day. Then the war which did so much evil destroyed those hopes too.

So Frania herself went ahead and brought Kasia from Tarnopol. She was worried about her in those uncertain days and wanted to have her daughter close to her. Her job as a maid at the German Officers Club brought her some money, and also special food rations. Frania started to sell the food for good money, and she was doing quite well, at least compared to other women in that time. She worried a lot. We had to be very careful. But, as the saying goes, the greatest darkness is behind the lantern. We succeeded. At least we survived.

After the Soviet liberation, when the Soviets finally liberated the town from the Nazis, we were able to leave the cupboard, but it was still very dangerous. Underground Ukrainian bands were still active. They murdered Poles and also the few surviving Jews. I met my present husband. He was twenty years older than me. His former wife and children had died in the ghetto. We decided to get together. I was young and inexperienced. I had my brother to protect, and Edek, my husband, was resourceful.

As soon as the war ended, we left with the first group of Polish displaced people for Wroclaw in Poland. From there I wrote to Frania and asked her to come and join us with her daughter. I wrote that we would help set her up in a new life.

I got only one answer from her. She wrote that she had by a miracle met Kasia's father again and that they had decided to get married. Because he was a Ukrainian, they had decided not to cross to Poland although they were going to leave Kolomyja. She forbade us to write to her again, because she did not want her husband to know that she had helped to hide Jews. And then all communication ended.

So much for our first letter. I hope that you sill stay in contact and that I will get to know more about the two of you. We must meet. It could be in England or Poland, or in Florida. Or maybe in Kolomyja, even that is now possible, although I am not sure that I could survive it emotionally.

Your happiness gives me great pleasure. Later, when I am sure that this letter has reached you, I will phone you.

Love,
Your Jula"

Leap for Life

There was a long long silence. So our cruel past had reached out to us again. In a way we had never expected. Once again I had to to reconsider Frania's actions. She had indeed been loyal and brave. Now I could truly appreciate it. To decide who to save, us or Jula and her brother, must have been a terrible moral dilemma for her. Particularly since she was a very religious woman, and did what her faith ordered her to do. She helped the oppressed because her faith told her to love her neighbour.

It had been hard for me to understand why she had not been able to take us in. But I am sure that she worried endlessly if she had made the right choice. She had to deal absolutely on her own with the problem Now I understood. But I was still puzzled why she had written to Jula that she did want want any more to do with Jews. She had not lacked for courage before; why had she then decided to cut herself off so completely from us ?

Maybe it was because she had finally been reunited with the father of her daughter and wanted to marry him, to give her daughter his name and his protection and to have a normal family. According to Jula, she had now become well off. Maybe she bought the man, about whom she had never spoken well, but whom she could obviously never fully forget? It is always difficult to know what the whole truth is. I needed to think it through. I needed to talk it all over with my brother. Maybe his analytic skill would help us resolve all these questions and understand her motives, which must have been complicated, and which could not have made her life easy.

Bezio, Jula, Frania and the Righteous Gentiles

But we should now be witnesses to the truth of Frania's courage, even if she herself will never know about it. We owe this to her memory. To the memory of her and the others who came into my life and into the lives of so many more like me. In contrast to the general opinion, these decent people were a whole army.

Because, without Frania and without Paulina, I would never have survived. And behind them stands the nameless Ukrainian peasant couple on the edge of the forest, who were there for me on the worst day of my life. And in Germany, Jekaterina and the German woman at the shoe factory who defended me against the claim of sabotage.

Then, of course, there was Witek, my husband and the father of my children. I and my daughters have him to thank for what our family became. Because despite the modest circumstances in which we had to live in post-war Poland, and despite the constant fear that we felt because of the totalitarian regime under which we, with forty million other Poles, had to live, we survived without too great harm. Because we existed for our family. And that succeeded wonderfully.

And what about my search. Did I not also meet so many decent people – *menschen* in the Yiddish. There is just no way to list all the people who created our chain of reunion. A chain of people of goodwill, thanks to whom Victor and I were able to find each other. From the anonymous clerk at the Warsaw archive, to Dasia, Professor Dov Noy, Renata, Rose and so many more.

These are the people who bring joy. These are the people who fill one with optimism that after all these years, after all we have been through, there are still such people. The people I have had the good fortune to encounter along my journey of life. There are surely more still to come.

Victor and I still have so much to tell each other, so much to work through. I hope we will do it all. Maybe together we will be able to write a book about all of this. It will be for our children, but not for them alone.

For it must be a reminder, to know but never to forget, and a rallying cry – *Never Again*.

Above all it should be a celebration of decent people everywhere. A celebration that must be both loud and determined, and a hope for the future.

Opposite: The reunion that came so late... the siblings
(photograph by Michael Austen)

My daughters with their own families on visits to Dairy Cottage

Left: Wiesia (kneeling centre) with daughter Basia, and son Piotr with his wife, Isa

Below: Kristina and her husband meeting Victor

Epilogue

Victor Zorza never made it to Poland. After an operation performed in the autumn of 1994, the year in which he and his sister had met after more than fifty years of separation, he felt worse rather than better.

The two of them had one more time together for a couple of months during the following summer at Dairy Cottage, but Victor's heart was by then very weak. At times he had to move around with the help of a wheeled walker. But he still spent his morning hours on the computer, working for the Russian hospice movement, drafting letters to people of influence who might be helpful to the cause when he would no longer be there.

"I'm not afraid to die," he used to tell his sister. "It was Jane who taught me that you shouldn't be afraid of it."

And what about his sister? Should she be sad or glad that they had finally met? Happy about the meeting, but sad that they would have so little time together. She was inclined to blame destiny. What could she say about the fact that fate had only allowed them to meet so late, after fifty three years apart? And so far had allowed them just two years together. Of that two years, really only three months that they had actually been together. How could that be enough to make up for the lifetime, for all those years during which they had been parted and knew nothing of each other? But for her there was more thankfulness than sorrow. Because they might just as easily have missed it all. She might have learnt about his survival too late, or not at all. And she was aware that thousands of Jewish families are waiting for a phone call like the one she got. All but a very few wait in vain.

When, in the summer of 1995, she was leaving Dairy Cottage for Poland, for her home, Victor accompanied her in his wheelchair to the end of the grounds. They embraced silently for a long time. They were aware that this might be the last time. They tried not to cry. When she got into the car which was to drive her to the airport, he raised his hand to her. He was sitting in his wheelchair, a small figure tormented by pain.

For her the scene echoed another goodbye, so long ago.

* * *

Richard's stepson, Arloc and partner Anne travelled from America for Victor's memorial day

Piotr and Isa came from Poland to join the crowd in the garden of Dairy Cottage.

Epilogue

Victor Zorza died on March 20, 1996. The funeral was modest, the ceremony simple with only ten people present, the closest family, his sister among them. A few months later the family arranged a "Victor Zorza Memorial Day" at Dairy Cottage. Nearly a hundred people came, including nine from Poland, his sister and her daughters and their families. Those who had not been able to come during his life, came after its end to honour his memory.

It was not a sad ceremony, it was a celebration. And the weather was fine, so the proceedings took place outside in the garden, just as a memorial birthday party for Jane had been held nearly twenty years before. Later, just as with Jane, his ashes were to be scattered in the garden. It was what he wanted.

There were toasts and speeches. Speeches by friends and former colleagues at the Guardian newspaper, by doctors from both the British and the Russian hospice movements, by a friend from his years in India, by neighbours and many, many others. The speeches were not sad. They were reflective, often tinged with humour. They were like Victor Zorza himself.

His sister also spoke a few words in her imperfect English. But she did not speak about the distinguished journalist everybody else knew. No, she talked about the young Polish schoolboy in the navy blue school uniform, who had carried an exercise book under his arm, and who used to write in that book halting but passionate verses - verses about brotherhood and the liberation of humankind.

Rut Wermuth Burak
Originally written in Poland 1996-98

**FINAŁ KONKURSU
PAMIĘCI POLSKO - ŻYDOWSKIEJ
O NAGRODĘ IM. DAWIDA BEN GURIONA**

PŁOŃSK 06. 09. - 10. 09. 1999 r.

**NAGRODA GŁÓWNA
IM. DAWIDA BEN GURIONA**
ufundowana przez Zarząd Miejski w Płońsku

dla Pani

RUT WERMUTH - BURAK

za pracę pt. *"Spotkałam ludzi..."*

W imieniu
Organizatorów Konkursu

Burmistrz Płońska
mgr Marian Michniewicz

W imieniu
Jury Konkursu

Przewodniczący
prof. Stanisław Sickierski

The certificate denoting the first prize in the Ben Gurion competition

Rut receiving her prize